Color

• Primary Colors 2

• Secondary Colors...7

• Colors Have Many Values 14

• Black and White...19

• Contrast..24

• Cool Colors and Warm Colors 29

• Complementary Colors 35

• Tertiary Colors 40

• Light Through a Prism 45

How to Teach Art to Children

Primary Colors

There are three **primary colors**: red, yellow and blue.
These colors are called primary colors because you can
mix them to create all the colors of the rainbow. These
colors create the foundation of the color wheel.

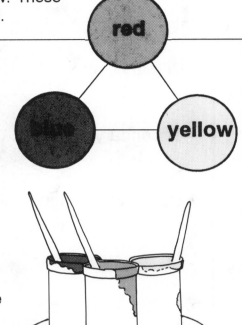

• Display the three primary colors and brainstorm
what we often associate with these colors.

> **yellow**-sun, hair, lemons
> **blue**-sky, water, jeans
> **red**-sunsets, flowers, apples

• Discuss how these colors have certain feelings
associated with them.

> **yellow** is cheerful
> **blue** is cool or sad
> **red** is angry or hot

• Invite students to look around the room to identify red objects.
Does red look the same each time we see it? Any color may be
altered by the amount of light that surrounds it. Take a red
sweater and compare how light or dark the red seems to be
depending on whether it is located in a dark closet or out in the
sunlight.

Literature references:

Mouse Paint by Ellen Stoll Walsh; Harcourt
Brace Jovanovich,1989.
Three white mice wander through jars of
primary colored paint. As they drip dry, they
leave puddles of paint that mix and create
new colors. The cut paper illustrations give
a graphic representation of how basic color
mixing works.

Color Dance by Ann Jonas; Greenwillow
Books, 1989.
This book uses the printer's basic colors of
magenta, yellow and cyan to discuss the
magic of color mixing.

Fine art examples to share with students:

Diamond Painting in Red, Yellow & Blue
Piet Mondrian
Mondrian is famous for creating geometric
designs. Can you find the three primary colors
he has used in this design? What other colors
did he choose to add? Do these colors enhance
his painting?

Woman Seated in an Armchair
Henri Matisse
Why does this picture attract your attention? Is it
the use of bright primary colors? Matisse loved
to use many bright colors in his paintings.

Dance at Bougival
Pierre Auguste Renoir
Find the primary colors in this painting. Why did
he use bright primary colors in the center of the
picture? Do these colors help attract your attention to the main characters?

How to Teach Art to Children

A Primary Color Quilt Design

Let's work together to investigate how primary colors interact in a geometric design.

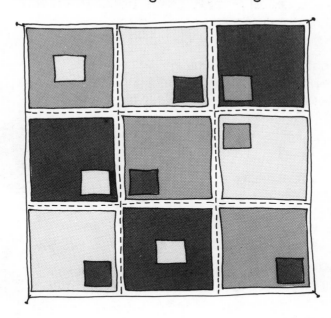

Divide the class into groups of 2-4 students.

Each group will need:
• one 27"(69 cm) square sheet of butcher paper folded
    into 9"(22.8 cm) squares
• three 9"(22.8 cm) square sheets of blue construction paper
• three 9"(22.8 cm) square sheets of red construction paper
• three 9"(22.8 cm) square sheets of yellow construction paper
• three 3"(7.5 cm) square sheets of blue construction paper
• three 3"(7.5 cm) square sheets of red construction paper
• three 3"(7.5 cm) square sheets of yellow construction paper
• glue

• Students meet in their groups gathered around the butcher paper grid. They place the larger primary-colored paper squares on the butcher paper. Experimenting with different arrangements should be encouraged. There is no "right" way to arrange the colors, it is entirely up to group tastes.

• Next the students place the smaller paper squares on top of the large squares. Many combinations may be tried before the students decide on the final arrangement.

• Students glue all squares in place when the arrangement is complete.

• Display all group designs when they are finished. Discuss the advantages of having several different results even though they began with the same color scheme.

One Color Art

Let students practice problem solving with
this art project.

What sort of subject might an artist choose
if he could use only one primary color to
create the picture? Could the artist create
a landscape or would it be wiser to make a
simple still life or design?

Encourage students to try three different
pictures using only ONE of the three
primary hues. Let them share the pictures
they feel work the best.

Each student will need:
• three pieces of 9" (22.8 cm) white art paper
• red or yellow or blue crayon
• black crayon

Allowing students to use a black crayon or
felt pen in addition to their choice of primary
color can add definition to the finished
work. The black can be used to outline
objects or add details.

Three Color Paint Job

Challenge students to create an interesting picture or design using the three primary colors: red, blue and yellow. Tempera paint and large white paint paper give students the resources to develop a striking picture that will make a colorful addition to the classroom and a rich topic for discussion about the effects created when these colors are used together.

What to put in the painting center:

• large white painting paper

• red, yellow and blue paint

• brushes in a variety of sizes

• a list of painting challenges

Suggested topics to challenge painters:

• Paint a beach ball rolling into the sea.

• Paint a rowboat on the lake on a sunny day.

• Paint all of the red, blue and yellow fruit you can think of.

• Paint an airplane zooming over a circus tent.

How to Teach Art to Children

Design an Individual Flag

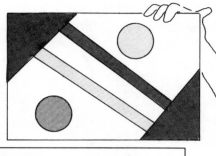

Each student will need:
• one 9" x 12" (22.8 x 30.5 cm) sheet of
white construction paper
• three 6" (15 cm) square sheets of
      construction paper in the primary
      colors of red, blue and yellow
• glue and scissors
• black crayon

Invite students to design their own per-
sonal flag using the three primary colors.
They may choose to cut their colored
squares into strips or circles or triangles.

Encourage them to experiment and try
several different designs before gluing the
pieces in place. They may add details
with a black crayon. Allow students time
to compare the different techniques used
and admire the colorful effects when they
are finished.

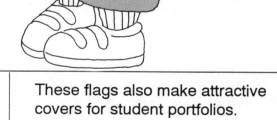

Flags can be attractively displayed along a string
stretched across one end of the classroom. Clothespins
hold the flags in place and are easy to move.

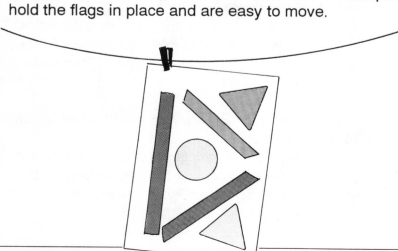

These flags also make attractive
covers for student portfolios.

How to Teach Art to Children

Secondary Colors

The primary colors can be mixed to create the **secondary colors** of orange, green and purple. If these colors are placed in a circle showing how they are related, you have created a color wheel.

Mix the Colors of the Color Wheel:
Use food coloring mixed with water in a clear plastic container set on an overhead projector to demonstrate how color mixing works. While you mix the colors, the students can document how primary colors interact by completing their own color wheel (See page 8).

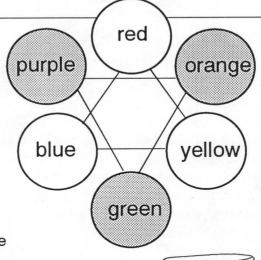

Tips on Successful Color Mixing:
-Pre-mix food coloring and water in glass jars for the three primary colors of red, blue and yellow.
-Use small plastic glasses or glass bowls to mix the secondary colors of orange, green and purple.
-Always begin with the lightest color and add the darker color one drop at a time.
-Mix one color at a time while the glass is sitting on the overhead projector so that the class can see the mixing as it happens on the screen.
-When all the mixing is complete, you will have represented all the colors on the color wheel. If you mix all the colors together, you will create a muddy black.

• **Literature References:**
Oh, Were They Ever Happy by Peter Spier; Doubleday & Co., 1978.
Involve students in this story of three children left at home for the day as they repaint the family home as a surprise for their parents.
The Mixed-Up Chameleon by Eric Carle; Harper & Row, 1975.
This delightful story reinforces the position of the colors on the color wheel.
The Very Hungry Caterpillar by Eric Carle; Philomel Books, 1969.
Enjoy Carle's tale while enjoying his colorful illustration style utilizing ALL the colors on the color wheel.

• **Fine art examples to share with students:**
Improvisation 31 (Sea Battle)
Wassily Kandinsky
The artist has used the colors of the color wheel in a very free way. There is the impression of movement created by the swirling colors. Does it remind you of a sea battle?

Sunday Afternoon on the Island of La Grande Jatte
Georges Seurat
All the colors of the color wheel are used by this artist in an interesting way. He put little dots of colors close together and your eye mixes the colors as you look at it.

Name: _____

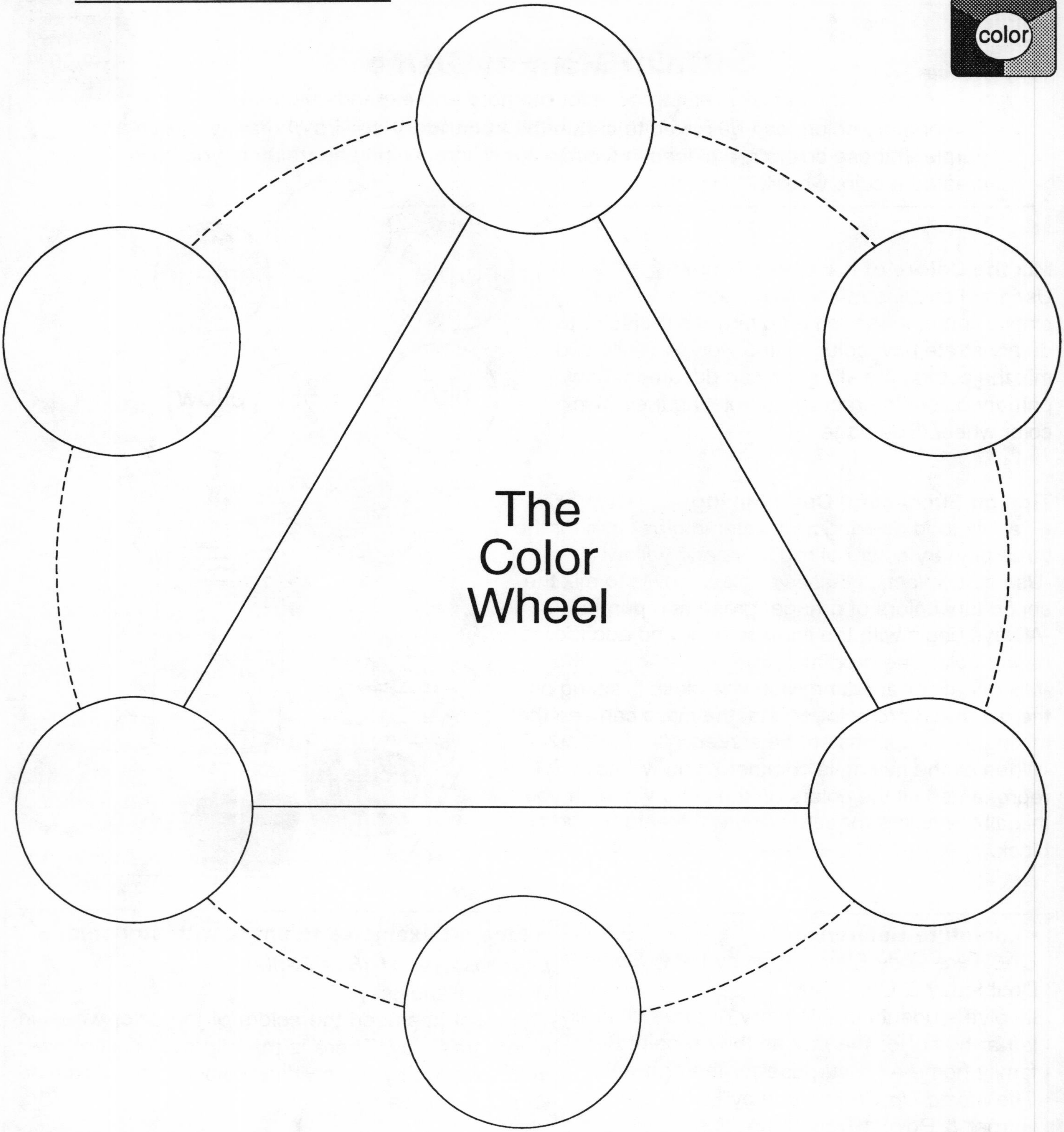

The
Color
Wheel

The primary colors are:

_____

_____

The secondary colors are:

_____

_____

8

How to Teach Art to Children

Color Memory Game

This activity reinforces color memory and expands student color awareness. Students of all ages can benefit from the strengthening of these skills. Divide your class into groups to play this game.

Each group will need:
- a selection of color strips
- larger paper samples in colors that match the color strips
- a coffee can

1. Pull one 9" x 12" (22.8 x 30.5 cm) sheet of colored construction paper from every color in your cupboard. Cut a 2"(5 cm) strip off the end of each colored sheet.

2. Place a number on the strip that corresponds to a number you place on the back of the larger sheet. Place the strips in a coffee can.

3. Lay the larger sheets in a random fashion on a table. Put a chair in front of the table but facing away from the table.

4. As several students sit facing the table, one student sits in the chair and picks a colored strip from the can. This student is to study the colored strip for a few seconds and place it back in the can after reporting to the group the number on the strip.

5. Then the student turns around and finds the matching color sheet on the table. After the color is chosen, the student must verify that the number matches the one on the strip by checking the number on the back of the sheet.

Color Mixing for All

Provide materials in a center where each student can
experience the magic of color mixing personally.

Materials needed:
• a pitcher of water
• 6 plastic drinking cups
• a spoon
• small-squeeze type bottle of food coloring in red, blue and yellow
• a copy of The Color Wheel (page 8) and a Color Experiments record sheet (page 11)
• a plastic tub or a sink to use for clean-up

A student comes to this center and mixes the food coloring and
water to create the colors on the color wheel. He/she can use
his/her color wheel form as a guide.

Remind the student that it is best to always begin with the
lightest color and add the darker color one drop at a time.

After each of the colors on the color wheel has been made,
encourage the students to experiment further to see what new
shades can be discovered. Have him/her document the new
color information on the experiment sheet on page 11.

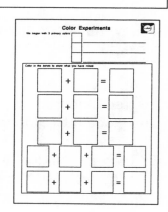

How to Teach Art to Children

Color Experiments

We began with 3 primary colors:

_____

_____

_____

Color in the boxes to show what you have mixed.

☐ + ☐ = ☐

☐ + ☐ = ☐

☐ + ☐ = ☐

☐ + ☐ + ☐ = ☐

☐ + ☐ + ☐ = ☐

How to Teach Art to Children

Mixing Gradations of Color

Students enjoy working with color mixing to produce
subtle variations in hues. Set up a center or area
where the basic color-mixing equipment is available
for students to use during the day.

Students work in the paint center to complete
the Changing Colors worksheet.

Materials:
• Changing Colors worksheet on page 13
• tempera paint premixed in the primary colors
  or watercolor trays
• brushes
• a plate on which to mix colors
• water and paper towels

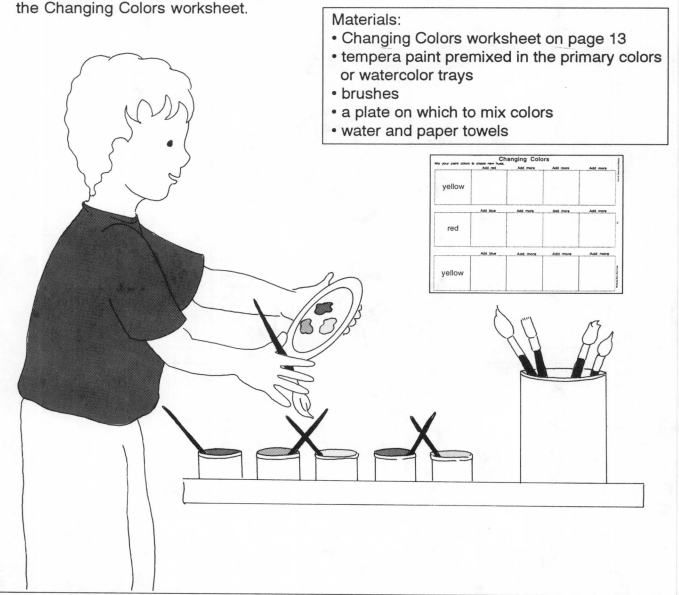

Follow-up:
Students may enjoy creating a design picture using the colored squares from their
worksheet. They cut the squares out and arrange them in interesting designs on
another sheet of paper. These projects can be striking additions to a student portfolio
and it offers a good opportunity to practice color mixing and experimentation.

How to Teach Art to Children

Changing Colors

Mix your paint colors to create new hues.

yellow	Add red	Add more	Add more	Add more

red	Add blue	Add more	Add more	Add more

yellow	Add blue	Add more	Add more	Add more

How to Teach Art to Children

Colors Have Many Values

The students will explore the different values of a color. Any hue or color on the color wheel may have an infinite number of values or tones. When colors are used at full value, they appear strong and bright. When colors are mixed with white paint or water they appear as muted, lighter tones.

Investigate the different values of a color by demonstrating to your students with watercolors.

Materials:
- a watercolor tray
- large watercolor brush
- dinner plate or tray (for mixing color)
- butcher paper

Spread a large sheet of butcher paper across the bulletin board. Use a large brush and mix a red watercolor puddle. Make a red blotch on the paper. Then add a brush of water to the red puddle on your tray. Now make another red blotch on the paper. Keep adding water to the red puddle and making blotches on the paper until you have samples of the color from its strongest, purest value to a muted pale value. Work your way through the other colors demonstrating how the strong hues can be diluted with water to paler tones.

Display the literature and fine art samples that you have gathered. Discuss with students the differences they perceive in illustration style and color choice. Some artists use colors with strong values to depict themes with strong emotional tone. Other artists prefer a muted, softer effect.

• Literature references:

Color Zoo
by Lois Ehlert;
Lippincott, 1989.
Vibrant primary colors and die cuts are featured in this clever book about basic shapes.

The Polar Express
by Chris Van Allsburg;
Houghton Mifflin,1985.
This story takes place at night so all the colors are muted by white or gray to obtain a softened look.

The Talking Eggs
by Robert D. San Souci,
illustrated by Jerry Pinkney;
Dial Books for Young Readers, 1989.
This book is a delightful combination of strong primary and muted color.

• Fine art examples: *strong color*

Cathedral
Hans Hofmann
This abstract painting features strong bright color and muted tones. Which tones have been muted? Why is it effective to use several values of one color in a painting?
Arabs Skirmishing in Mountains
Eugène Delacroix
The artists use of vivid color adds to the intensity of this scene.

muted color

The Artist and His Mother
Arshile Gorky
The pale, muted colors soften this painting. What was the artist trying to convey?
Woman Ironing
Edgar Degas
This picture uses gray and muted tones to picture this woman working. How would this picture make you feel if it were painted in bright yellows, reds, and greens?

Light and Dark

Working together with a partner, students demonstrate that any color can have more than one value.

Divide the class into groups of 2 students.
Each group will need:
• a 12" (30 cm) square piece of construction paper
• a box of crayons
• a 13" (33 cm) square of black construction paper for a frame

Demonstrate how to fold the construction paper into 16 squares.

The group members are to choose from their box of crayons and color each of the 16 boxes, but they must use each crayon TWICE.

• The first time they use a crayon they are to color the box of their choice as DARK as possible.

• Then they are to choose another box and color with the same crayon, but this time, color as LIGHTLY as possible.

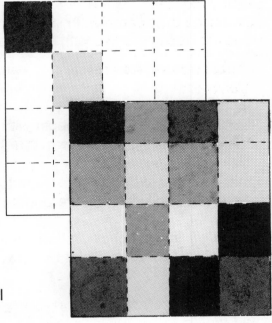

The task is complete when all boxes are filled with color. Students enjoy discussing which colors look best side by side and deciding how the changes in color placement effect the feel of the design.

Create a frame for each square by gluing it to the black square of construction paper. Display all the squares on the bulletin board. Students may want to create additional squares to add to this display. If squares are arranged close together, it begins to look like a colorful quilt. This would be an ideal time to share literature about quilts and the history of quilt making.

The Patchwork Quilt by Valerie Flournoy; Dial Books, 1985.

Mixing Colors with White

Students need:
- a copy of the Mixing Colors with White form on page 17
- a set of tempera colors mixed in the primary and secondary colors
- white tempera paint
- a brush
- a plate on which to mix colors
- access to a sink
- paper towels

The form is completed by each student in his/her free time or during a center experience.

Encourage them to begin with a small puddle of red paint. Paint the circle marked red on the form.

Add one drop of white paint to the red puddle. Mix this new color on the plate and paint the next circle in line.

Now add another drop of white paint to this same puddle of color. Paint the next circle with this lighter tone.

Add one more drop of white paint to this same puddle. Now you have the lightest tone of all. Paint the next circle on the form.

Follow this procedure for the other colors on the color wheel. Students will have best results if they rinse their plate before working with a new color.

Colors of the Color Wheel

Mixing Colors with White

	Add one drop of white	Add another drop	Add another drop
red 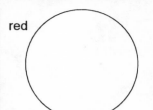	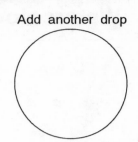	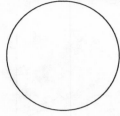	
orange 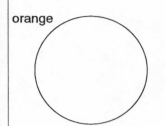	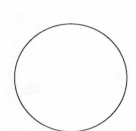	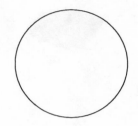	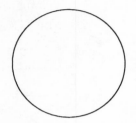
yellow 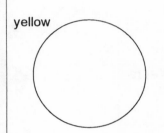	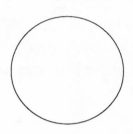	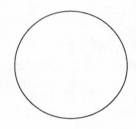	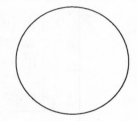
green 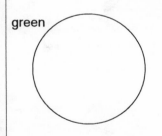	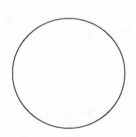	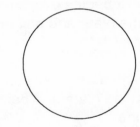	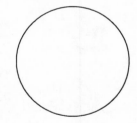
blue 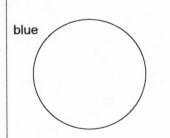	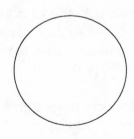	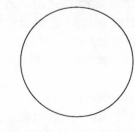	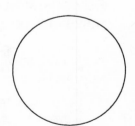
purple 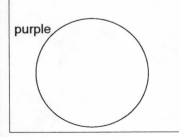	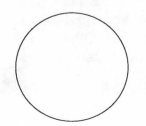	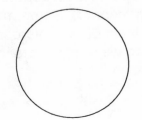	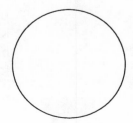

How to Teach Art to Children

Watercolor Washout

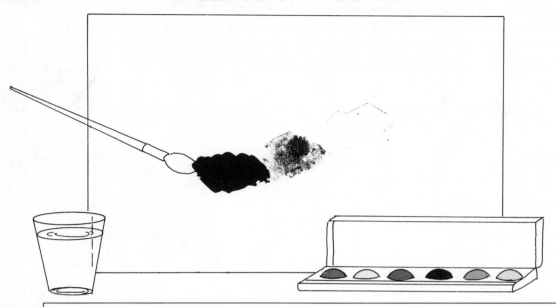

Each student needs:
• a watercolor tray with the primary and secondary colors
• a medium size brush that holds enough water to create wash effects
• 12" x 18" (30 x 45.7 cm) white art paper
• a plastic plate

The student begins by mixing as dark a red as possible on the plate and paints a section on the left side of his/her paper.

Then he/she adds one brush full of water to the red puddle on the plate and paints another section next to the first one.

He/she adds another brush full of water to the puddle on the plate, mixes it and paints another section on the paper. Little by little, the red color is diluted with water and the student will end up with a pale pink wash.

Then the student cleans up the plate and begins this process with the next color on the color wheel. It is entirely up to the student to arrange these colors in a pleasing manner. Some may choose to just make straight lines of color across the paper. Others may choose to wind the colors in and out creating a free-form design.

Black and White

color

Black is the darkest color and white is the lightest color. Because of that extreme, they offer a striking contrast when used together. That contrast creates a strong visual image. Students should also be aware that existing between black and white are an infinite number of grays.

Let's begin our investigation of black and white by creating a design using black and white construction paper . Each student will create a design.

Each student will need:
• a sheet of 9" x 12" (22.8 x 30.5 cm) black construction paper
• a sheet of 9" x 6" (22.8 x 15 cm) white construction paper
• scissors, paste and a pencil

1. Draw several light pencil lines from the top to the bottom of the white paper.

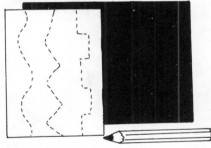

2. Cut the white paper on the pencil lines. Spread out the white strips across the black paper.

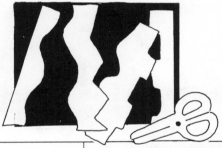

3. Experiment with variations and then paste the white strips down.

•**Literature references:**

Ben's Trumpet by Rachel Isadora; Greenwillow, 1979.
Why did the illustrator use black and white in this book instead of bright colors? How does she create the feeling of movement and rhythm with these pictures?

The Garden of Abdul Gasazi by Chris Van Allsburg; Houghton, 1979.
The illustrator has used only pencil to create these pictures full of detail. Examine the pages to see how the darks and lights create contrasts that attract your attention.

•**Fine art examples to share with students:**

The Scream
Edvard Munch

The Three Trees
Rembrandt van Rijn

Guernica
Pablo Picasso

Reconciliation Elegy
Robert Motherwell

All of these works of art are fine examples of how strong black and white can be when used together in a painting. The themes tend to be dramatic and the visual image powerful.

How to Teach Art to Children

Black and White and In-between

Let's investigate the tones of gray that exist between black and white. This activity involves the creation of a light to dark scale and requires careful mixing of colors. It is a good activity to share with a friend.

Divide the class so that each person has a partner.
Each group will need:
• a Black, White and Gray form on page 21
• white tempera paint
• black tempera paint
• a brush
• water for cleaning the brush
• paper towels
• a plate for mixing colors

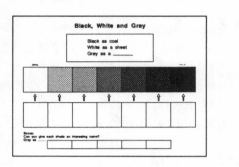

The student partners work together to complete this light to dark scale.

They paint in the white box first. Then they paint the black box.

Now they must mix white and black to create a middle tone. It is always best to begin the mixing with the lightest tone first. So they should put white on their plate and add black one drop at a time to create the gray that they feel should be in the middle.

Then they can continue to mix gradations of gray and fill in the other four boxes.

Students might now assign names to the grays they have developed. What sort of feeling is generated by each of these values?

Older students may want to attempt this same activity using black crayon instead of paint.

How to Teach Art to Children

Black, White and Gray

Black as coal
White as a sheet
Gray as a _____

Black

White

Bonus:
Can you give each shade an interesting name?
Gray as ....

Positive and Negative Designs
Students create positive-negative paper designs.

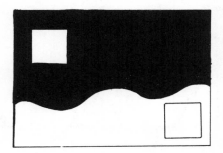

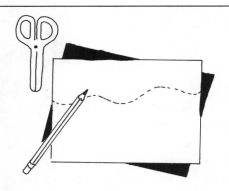

Each student will need:
• a sheet 6" x 9" (15 x 22.8 cm) construction paper in black and one in white
• 2 gray 2" (5 cm) squares
• scissors, glue and a pencil

Students draw a line from the top to the bottom of the white paper. This line can have bumps, curves, angles, scallops or any other design.

The student cuts on the line he/she has drawn. The two parts of the white paper are pasted together.

Paste one of these white sections on the black sheet of construction paper. The positive-negative design has now been created. The interesting thing about this type of design is that it can be viewed by concentrating on the positive side (white) or by concentrating on the negative side (black).

Now add the gray element to the design. A gray box is to be added to each side of the design. Students should experiment with different effects.

This type of project is successful as a part of an independent art center because students enjoy experimenting with the different shapes and line types that they can use. Allow them time and materials to create several different versions.

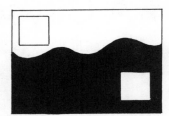

Share with your class the picture book
Round Trip
by Ann Jonas; Scholastic, 1983.
This book does a fine job of acquainting students with the concept of positive and negative design in art. She uses black and white to create striking illustrations.

**Independent
Student
Project**

Paint Center

Provide a paint area for children to experiment with black, white and gray paint. They may choose to paint free-form designs or they may decide to paint pandas, zebras and skunks.

It is helpful for certain children to have some beginning structure in a paint center. You might provide a list of paint jobs they could experiment with that fit the theme of black and white and gray. Reproduce this list to help students get started.

Snowman in a Snowstorm
Cat on a Foggy Day
A Cityscape at Night
Dark Winter Night
Train in a Tunnel
An Airplane in a Cloud

       How to Teach Art to Children

Contrast

color

Contrast is the degree of difference between colors or tones in a piece of artwork. Using contrasting colors next to each other in a picture can help to frame a point of focus. It is important to define that focus point and set it apart from the background so that the picture is interesting to view and the main interest point is clearly visible.

Have a basket of items brought from home to share with students. Lay each item on a different color background. Experiment with several different backgrounds to see which color offers the best contrast.

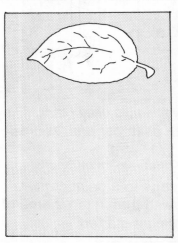
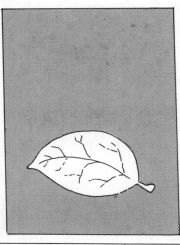

• Literature references:

The Ghost-Eye Tree by Bill Martin Jr., with illustrations by John Archambault.
Why are the illustrations in this story so dramatic? The strong contrasting colors used by the illustrator have contributed to the drama of the story. The dark backgrounds and the strong light cast on the characters give the book a mysterious feeling.

When I Was Young In the Mountains by Cynthia Rylant and Illustrated by Diane Goode.
Enjoy the limited palette that Diane Goode has used to create these sensitive illustrations. Notice that despite the muted colors, she has utilized contrasting values to set her characters apart from the background design. Often her characters are dressed in white or light colors and they are surrounded by dark browns or blues.

• Fine art examples to share with students:

The return from the hunt
or
The Country Wedding
Pieter Brueghel
Brueghel uses light and dark to create dramatic paintings that attract our attention. Encourage students to be aware of how he uses darks and lights side by side to maximize the contrast.

The Feast of Belshazzar
Rembrandt
This artist is well known for his use of light and dark areas. The Feast is a good example of how effective he is in planning a painting with good contrast.

Ginevra de 'Benci
Leonardo da Vinci
Portraits by this artist are well loved because they are so lifelike and natural. This portrait is typical of the way he highlights the subjects by surrounding them in a contrasting tone.

Pick Contrasting Colors

Students will manipulate colored cards to discover
which colors appear to be contrasting colors.

Divide the class into groups of 2-4 students.
Materials for each group:
• a 5" (13 cm) square of construction paper in red,
orange, yellow, green, blue, purple, black and white
• a 2" (5 cm) square of construction in the same colors
• a copy of the Contrasting Colors worksheet on page 26
• crayons

1. The students work in their groups manipulating
the color cards. Which color combinations appear to offer the strongest contrast?

Students begin by laying out all eight of the
larger squares. Then they place one of the
smaller squares in the center of each larger one.
They keep rearranging the smaller squares until
they find the three best contrasting combinations.

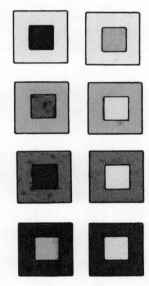

2. They use their crayons to record those
combinations on their worksheet.

3. The next job is to decide which three combinations of colors represent samples of least contrast. Students manipulate the cards and then
record their choices on the worksheet.

After the separate groups have compiled their lists of contrasting color
combinations, it is interesting to compare the results.

• Did the groups choose the same combinations?

• Are there combinations of colors that are not
contrasting but that are still pleasing to students?

         How to Teach Art to Children

Contrasting Colors

Best contrast:

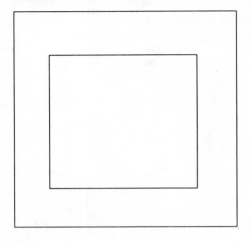 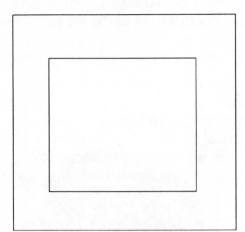 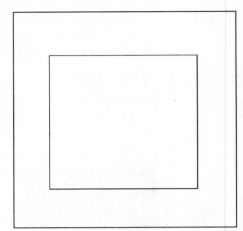

Least contrast:

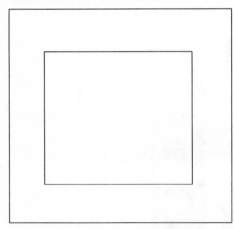 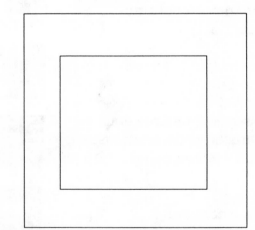 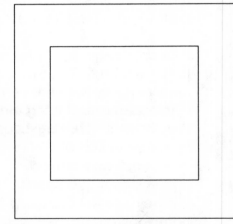

Favorite combinations:

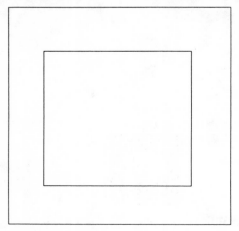 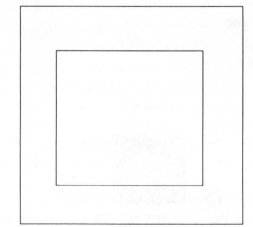 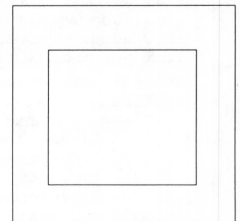

Contrasting Backgrounds

Let students experience how contrasting colors affect their artwork. This lesson offers students the opportunity to try several different backgrounds for their illustration. They should have the responsibility of choosing the background that achieves the effect they desire.

  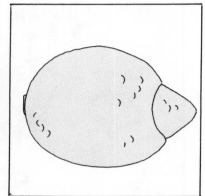

Materials that each student will need access to:
• three 3" (7.5 cm) squares of white drawing paper
• a selection of 6" (15 cm) colored construction paper in all available colors
• pencil and crayons
• scissors and paste

1. Students draw three things things on the white drawing paper: an apple, plum and a lemon.

2. They cut out the pictures.

3. They experiment with background color by laying their fruit pictures on several different colors of construction paper. Which color best sets off each of the fruits? They choose the ones they like the best and paste the fruits on them.

yellow on yellow = poor contrast

yellow on purple = strong contrast

yellow on red = good contast, warm colors

Strip Art

Students can experiment with color preferences and design ideas to develop a piece of art work that illustrates the principle of contrasting colors.

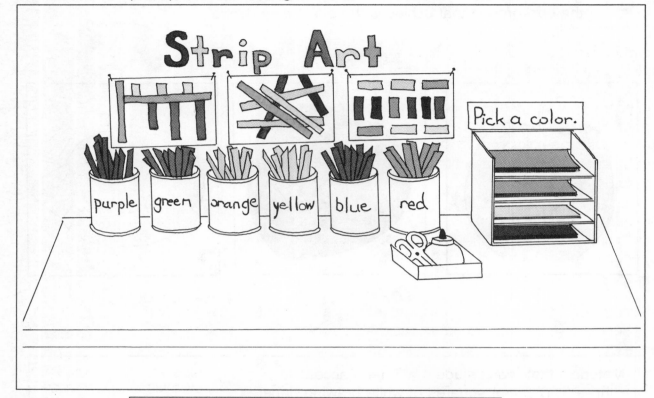

Set up a center containing:
• background sheets- 9" x 12" (22.8 x 30.5 cm) construction paper in the colors of the color wheel plus black and white
• 1" x 12" (2.5 x 30.5 cm) construction paper strips in all of the same color choices
• paste
• scissors

Students begin by choosing three to five colored strips and a background sheet from the selection of colors available. They may need to return to the center and get more strips as they finalize on their design. Discuss with students some things they might consider in making their color choices. Do they want to create a design that has contrast or do they want a design that is subtle?

They can try many different combinations of color and pattern before they paste down their finished arrangement.

Cool Colors and Warm Colors

Blue, green and purple are often labeled cool colors. Yellow, orange and red are called the warm colors on the color wheel. How can colors give this impression of temperature? Is it based on scientific fact or is it based on how those colors make us feel?

Open a discussion with students about ways to categorize colors. Suggest that today the way you are going to categorize color is by the way it makes you feel. You are going to go through your paper scrap box or your collection of color chip cards and categorize them into two groups: warm colors and cool colors. Use the color wheel as a point of reference so that you can be sure you have placed each of these in one of the categories.

After you have divided your color samples into two piles, list all of the colors on a chart divided into the cool section and the warm section. Look again at the color wheel and notice how it has been divided by these categories.

Warm and cool colors do evoke emotional responses. People often label colors with unusual names because of these responses. Color names can be dramatic. A visit to a paint store can help you compile a long list of interesting color names. Bring back to class samples of the color chip cards to share with students.

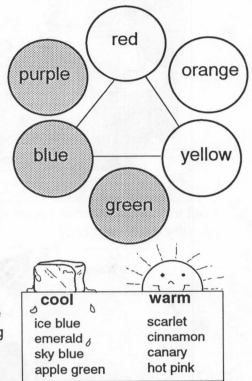

cool	warm
ice blue	scarlet
emerald	cinnamon
sky blue	canary
apple green	hot pink

cool palette	warm palette
• **Literature references** *Owl Moon* by Jane Yolen, illustrated by John Schoenherr, 1987. The illustrator has chosen cool colors (even cool warm colors) to depict a winter scene on a moonlit night.	*Arrow to the Sun* by Gerald McDermott; Viking Press, 1974. Compare the illustrations in this book that use all warm colors with the illustrations that are done in cool hues. How do the warmer tones fit the theme?
• **Fine art samples** *The Old Guitarist* Pablo Picasso *The Long Leg* Edward Hopper *Houses in Provence* Paul Cezanne *The Basin at Deauville* Raoul Dufy These artists have used cool palettes to convey different feelings. Picasso's *Guitarist* projects a melancholy mood. Cezanne and Hopper have used cool colors to lend a sense of serenity to scenes from nature. Dufy creates an effective abstract by using cool blues with a touch of red for contrast.	*Farmhouse in Provence, Arles* Vincent van Gogh Warm colors lend a feeling of heat or intensity to this landscape. You can feel the warmth of that sun radiating off the trees and the land. *Table Set in a Garden* Pierre Bonnard The artist has used warm and cool colors together to create a sense of contrast between the coolness of the shade and the warm invitation to the table.

           How to Teach Art to Children

Colorful Collage

Students work together with warm and
cool colors to develop a collage.

Divide the class into groups of 2-4 students.
Each group will need:
- magazines
- a 36" (91 cm) square sheet of white
  butcher paper
- scissors and paste

Fold the white butcher paper into fourths.
Identify each section:

- **All Warm**

- **All Cool**

- **Mostly Warm with
  a Cool Accent**

- **Mostly Cool with
  a Warm Accent**

Each group searches through the magazines looking for patches of color that fit one of the
categories. They may tear out or cut out samples. They may choose to overlap the pieces
as they paste them in place or they may leave white spaces in-between. It is only important
that the students enjoy the process and are pleased by the finished color pattern.

When all groups have finished, it is interesting to compare the final effects and identify the
different sections of color. A discussion might develop around which effect the students
prefer. Does using cool and warm colors together create a more interesting picture?

The papers may be cut into separate sections and framed as a display in the classroom.

How to Teach Art to Children

Mix Cool and Warm Colors

Let's experiment with the colors on the color wheel again.

Begin with red. Red is a warm color.
Is it possible to develop a "cool red"? What would we have to add?
When blue is added to red a "cool red" is created. However, when yellow is added to red, a "warmer red" appears.

Each student will need:
- a Warm It Up-Cool It Down form on page 32
- tempera paint in the colors of the color wheel
- a brush
- water
- a plate for mixing colors

Students will have the opportunity in this lesson to experiment with color mixing to create variations of the basic color wheel hues. They follow the steps on the **Warm It Up-Cool It Down** worksheet to create cooler tones by the addition of a primary cool color and warmer tones by the addition of a primary warm color.

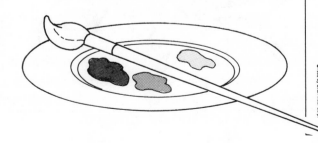

Warm It Up-Cool It Down

Warm or Cool?	Warmer?	Cooler?
red		
yellow		
blue		
orange		
green		
purple		

After students have completed the **Warm It Up-Cool It Down** form, they may enjoy painting a picture in the Paint Center that gives them an opportunity to use the colors they have been mixing.

Warm It Up-Cool It Down

Warm or Cool?	Warmer?	Cooler?
red		
yellow		
blue		
orange		
green		
purple		

My Favorite Palette

After students have experimented with mixing variations of the primary and secondary colors, discuss which color combination they prefer. Explain that most artists have a preferred palette that they use again and again. Let students experiment with various combinations to discover their favorite combinations.

Set up a paint center with the following instructions:

Pick a Palette

Paint a picture with the palette you like the best.

1. Warm colors only

2. Cool colors only

3. Warm colors with a cool accent

4. Cool colors with a warm accent

How to Teach Art to Children

Tissue Paper Collage

Set up an area for students where they can choose materials to complete a tissue paper collage using the palette of colors they have identified as their favorite.

- Students may create desert pictures using warm colors.
- They may choose to do underwater scenes that use mostly cool colors.
- They may prefer to do a flower picture using the colors in combination.
- Perhaps they will create free-form designs.

*Pick your colors.
1. Make a design.
2. Brush on starch.*

Materials:
- tissue paper cut into 2" (5 cm) strips
  (red, orange, yellow, green, blue and purple)
- liquid starch in a bowl
- wide brushes
- large white construction paper
- black felt tip pens for adding details

Students may use the strips as whole pieces or they may like to tear or cut the strips into smaller pieces. When the students have decided on the effect they want to achieve, they adhere the tissue to the construction paper by brushing on starch. When the starch and tissue have dried, students may add details to their picture with black felt tip pen.

Eric Carle's style of illustration typifies the use of bold color and collage. Sharing the illustrations in his books can motivate students to try new themes with this technique.

The Grouchy Ladybug, Crowell, 1977.
The Very Hungry Caterpillar, Philomel Books, 1969.

How to Teach Art to Children

Complementary Colors

Complementary colors are pairs of colors that sit opposite one another on the color wheel. Children need to experiment with these colors to understand that they are powerful when used together. Complementary colors appear to vibrate when placed side by side.

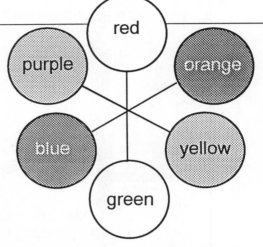

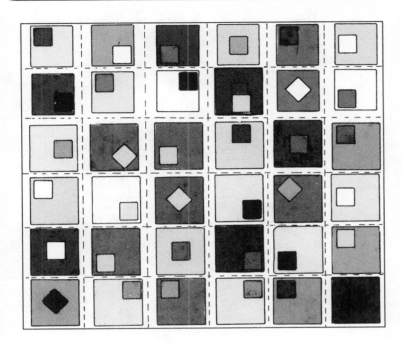

Let's experiment with complementary colors to see how they work. Display the color wheel and discuss where complementary colors are located. Draw lines between these pairs of colors to emphasize their relationship.

We will need the following materials:

- a 36" (91.4 cm) square sheet of butcher paper folded into 6" (15 cm) boxes
- 6" (15 cm) squares of construction paper

6 - red	6 - green
6- orange	6 - blue
6 - yellow	6 - purple

- 2" (5 cm) squares of construction paper

6- red	6 - green
6 - orange	6 - blue
6 - yellow	6 - purple

- straight pins

Each student gets one large construction paper square and one small construction paper square. Pin the butcher paper on the bulletin board. Each student pins up his/her large colored square onto the butcher paper where they choose.

When all the large squares have been placed on the butcher paper, students must pin their small squares within the complementary colored squares. It can be positioned anywhere within the square.

- **Literature References:**

Eyes of the Dragon
by Margaret Leaf, illustrated by Ed Young, Lothrop, Lee & Shepard, 1987.
The illustrator has used strong primary colors and often placed complementary colors side-by-side which results in powerful pictures that almost seem to move off the page.

- **Fine art examples to share with students:**

Street, Dresden
Ernst Ludwig Kirchner

Charing Cross Bridge
André Derain

Complementary color schemes in these paintings help make powerful statements about the subject matter. Can you tell how these artists feel about the cities they are painting?

35

Colors Interact

Involve students in a free exploration time using colored squares of paper.
Let them practice what they've learned about how colors interact.

Divide the class into groups of 2-4 students.

1. Set out a box of colored 6" squares for each
group. Include all the colors represented on the
color wheel.

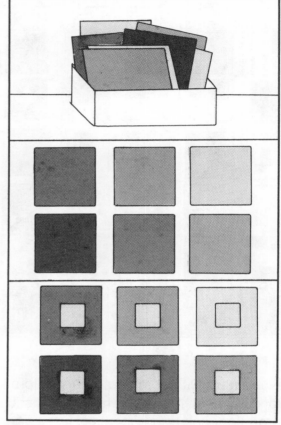

2. The groups are asked to organize their color
samples into complementary color pairs.

3. Then each group is given ten 2" (5 cm) gray
squares. They are invited to place the gray
squares on the colored squares.

Students will be surprised to discover that two gray boxes will appear to be of a
different value when sitting side by side on complementary colors. It is important that
students realize that the background that surrounds a color affects and alters that
color in some way. Give the groups time to experiment with other color combinations.
Also provide students with black and white boxes to use in their experiments.

Each group of students should be encouraged to list three things they have discovered
about colors and how they work together from this experiment. It is interesting to compare among the groups and discuss the findings.

How colors work:

1. Complementary colors are
strong side by side.
2. Background colors
affect other colors used.

How to Teach Art to Children

Complementary Rip and Paste

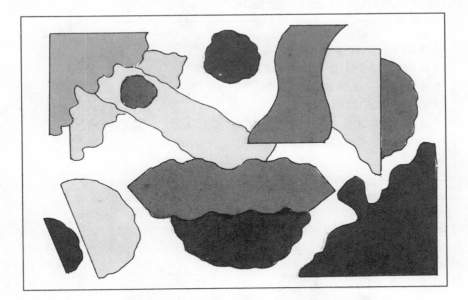

Each student will need:
• 9" x 12" (22.8 x 30.5 cm) white construction paper
• 4" (7.5 cm) squares in every color on the color wheel
• paste

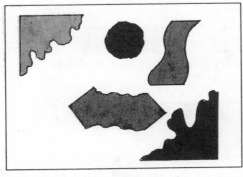

The student begins this project by ripping off a piece of each colored square. This piece may be small or it may even mean just ripping the piece in half. Lay all the pieces on the white construction paper in a random fashion.

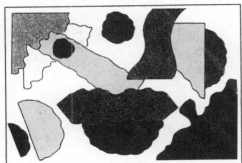

Now comes the challenge. **Only complementary colors may touch each other.** So all the scraps must be rearranged.

When the design is complete, the pieces may be pasted in place.

How to Teach Art to Children

Peek and Paint

Students use the previous activity to assist in the creation of an interesting painting emphasizing complementary colors.

Each student will need:
- a finished **Rip and Paste** project
- a paint easel and paints
- large painting paper
- a 6" (15 cm) square of paper cut with a 5" frame inside to create a peek-through frame

The student uses his/her "peek" frame to select an interesting part of the Rip and Paste design. He/she tapes the frame in place.

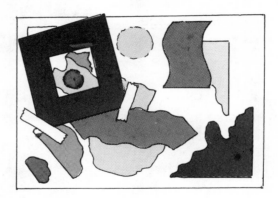

Now the student paints what he/she sees in the frame. The finished painting will be an interesting free-form design.

Complementary Turn About

This cut and paste activity results in a striking design for the cover of a folder or for a portfolio front. The challenge for each student is to select papers in complementary colors

Each student will need:
- four 6"(15 cm) squares of construction paper in the same color
    (Provide a choice from all the colors of the color wheel.)
- a 12"(30.5 cm) square of construction paper
    (The color must be complementary to the smaller squares.)
- pencils, paste and scissors

Fold the large square into quarters.

Draw an "interesting" line through one small square paper and then cut on that line. Take one piece of the cut square and paste it in one section of the large complementary square. They have now created a positive-negative design in that section.

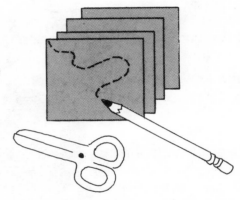

Now the student is to duplicate this design in each of the remaining sections of the large square. They can use the piece of construction paper that was left from the first square as a pattern.

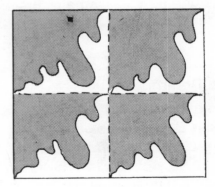

Challenge:
Each time the student pastes the cut form into a section, he/she may rotate the design so that it turns around the center point.

The completed result is a design that is a striking use of complementary colors and a simple repetitive design.

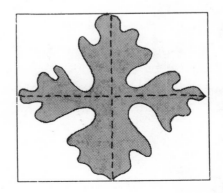

How to Teach Art to Children

Tertiary Colors

Tertiary colors are colors created by the mixing of secondary colors. Mixing these hues tends to create colors with a grayish or muted effect. This is an important technique for students to be aware of and practice in their painting activities.

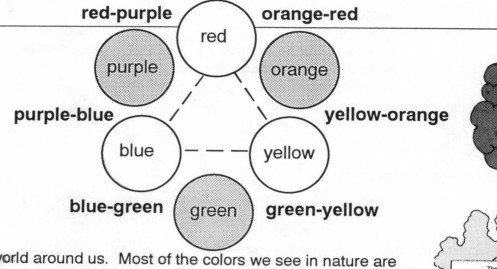

Let's look at the world around us. Most of the colors we see in nature are tertiary colors. Only occasionally do you see a primary or secondary color in full strength.

Take a class walk around the playground or the neighborhood to become aware of and categorize the colors in our world. Arm each student with a copy of the Tertiary Color Wheel on page 41. They may color in the wheel before the walk. As the students identify the colors in their environment, they list what they see by each tertiary color. Can they find two examples for each color?

• **Literature References:**

The Legend of Scarface
by Robert San Souci; Doubleday, 1978. Notice how the illustrator has mixed his hues to create the colors of nature. The tertiary colors are used instead of strong primary colors. The use of light around dark colors has also created a fine example of contrast.

Pumpkin Pumpkin
by Jeanne Titherington; Greenwillow, 1986. Blending of colors by using layers of colored pencils creates soft, tertiary colors. Note how layering adds depth and shape to forms.

• **Fine art examples to share with students:**

Boys in a Pasture
Winslow Homer
The Equatorial Jungle
Henri Rousseau
These artists have chosen very different styles but have both used tertiary colors to represent scenes from nature.

A Corner of the Moulin de la Galette
Henri de Toulouse-Lautrec

Toulouse seems always to have had a fondness for the subdued effect of tertiary colors in his posters and paintings. He uses the grayish blue-green and purple-blue often as a background for his colorful characters.

The Tertiary Color Wheel
Can you tell the difference between these colors?

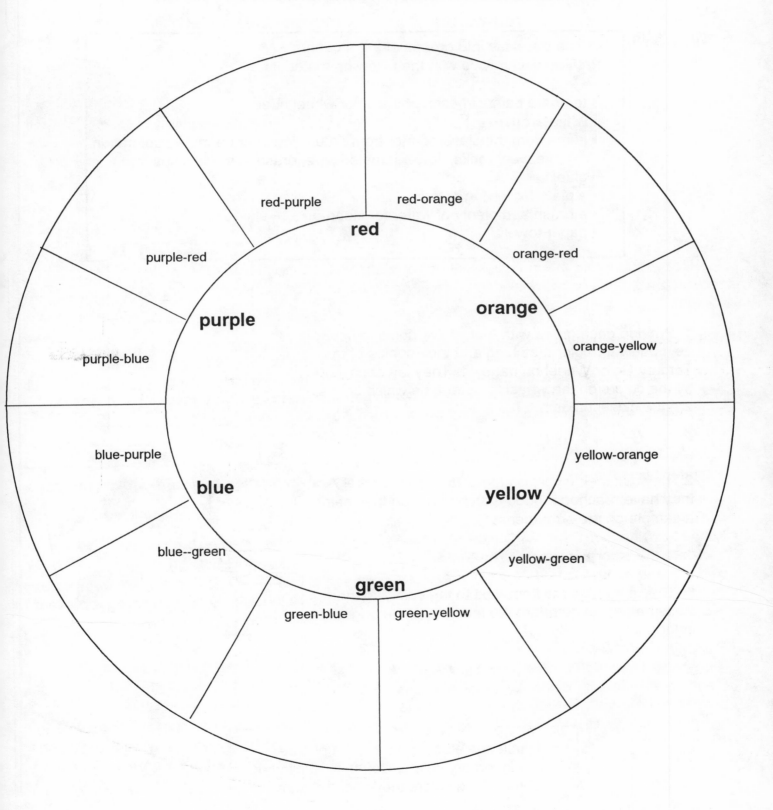

color

red-purple

red-orange

red

purple-red

orange-red

purple

orange

purple-blue

orange-yellow

blue-purple

yellow-orange

blue

yellow

blue--green

yellow-green

green

green-blue

green-yellow

Mix Secondary Colors

Let's work together and mix our secondary colors and
see if we can match the colors we see in nature.

Divide the class into groups of 2-4 students.
Provide each group with the following materials:

- tempera paints in each of the color wheel hues
- white art paper
- items from the classroom or from nature that have a muted coloration
    (leaves, rocks, flowers, rusted pipe, erasers, wood chips, etc.)
- glue
- a plate for mixing colors
- a brush and plenty of water for clean-up
- paper towels

1. Provide each group with four or five items to use
as models for color matching and their copies of the
Tertiary Color Wheel on page 41. They lay each item
by the colors on the wheel to determine which colors
are the closest match.

2. They mix their colors on the plate until they feel
they have reached a good match and then they paint
a sample on the art paper.

3. They may glue the item next to the color, so that
classmates can compare the match and the original
color.

Challenge students to paint a picture
using tertiary colors. Can they duplicate
some of the colors they see in nature?

Colored Pencil Blending

Share books with students where the illustrator has chosen colored pencil as an art medium. Help them to see how pencil layering of primary and secondary colors can achieve a muted, teritiary effect.

Each student will need:
• colored pencils
• The Tertiary Color Wheel (page 41)
• art paper
• time to experiment

1. Students use the technique of layering one color of pencil over another colored layer of pencil. They need to practice using a light and consistent pressure on the pencil to achieve successful layering.

Have the students complete the Tertiary Color Wheel form. This exercise gives them time to practice their technique with the colored pencils.

2. When students have experience with the pencils give them art paper and let them try their hand at creating a picture using the pencils and tertiary color. Provide them with simple objects from nature to draw: a piece of fruit, an interesting leaf, several interesting rocks, potted plants, etc.

Paint a Landscape

Plan to give students time at a painting center where they can experiment with paints and mixing paints to achieve different tones and hues.

Materials that makes color mixing possible:
- a plate or tray for mixing colors so that the color can be blended before putting it on the paper
- water for cleaning brushes before mixing a new color
- inexpensive paper for experimenting (perhaps even recycled newspapers)

Make a list of problems you would like students to solve at the paint center. Landscape painting lends itself to many interesting probem-solving tasks.

Paint yourself standing by the river.

Paint yourself in a boat at sea.

Paint a tree blowing in a storm.

Paint a hill with trees on the top and houses at the bottom.

Paint a child hiding in the grass.

Paint a dog under a tree digging for a bone.

Light Through a Prism

Intermediate students need to know that light is made up of a band or a spectrum of color. These colors travel in waves and each color has a different wavelength. You can prove this by letting light pass through a three-sided piece of glass called a prism. The light that appears clear is changed into seven colors: red, orange, yellow, green, blue, violet and indigo as it passes through the surface of the prism.

Share with students the basic facts:

• The basic colors of light are different from the basic colors of paint. Color mixing with paint is a process involving blending of the three primary colors of red, yellow and blue.

• Color mixing with light is a different process. Light appears to be clear as we see it around us. However, if you pass light through a prism, it breaks it down into a whole band of colors: red, orange, yellow, green, blue, indigo and violet.

• Red, green and violet-blue are the primary colors of light. We can make the other combinations by mixing those.

• The rainbow demonstrates this breakdown of light into a spectrum of color. The raindrop acts like a prism and shatters the light apart into its various wavelengths.

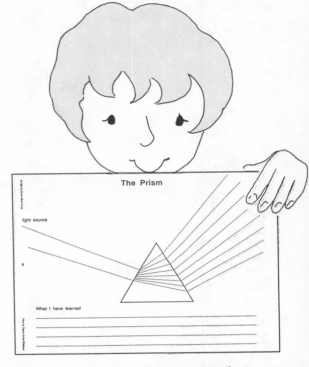

Use a prism to demonstrate that these facts are true. The students can record their findings on The Prism form on page 46.

• **Literature References:**

The Magic of Color by Hilda Simon; Lothrop, Lee & Shepard Books, 1981.
This nonfiction book provides a clear explanation of how color appears in our world. This is a good reference books for all the basic color concepts.

• **Fine art examples to share with students:**

Street Light
Giacomo Balla
This painting is interesting to share with students when you are discussing the basic colors of light and how they can be broken down by a prism. This artwork depicts a streetlight that breaks light down into a shower of color, too. Let students compare this light and a prism.

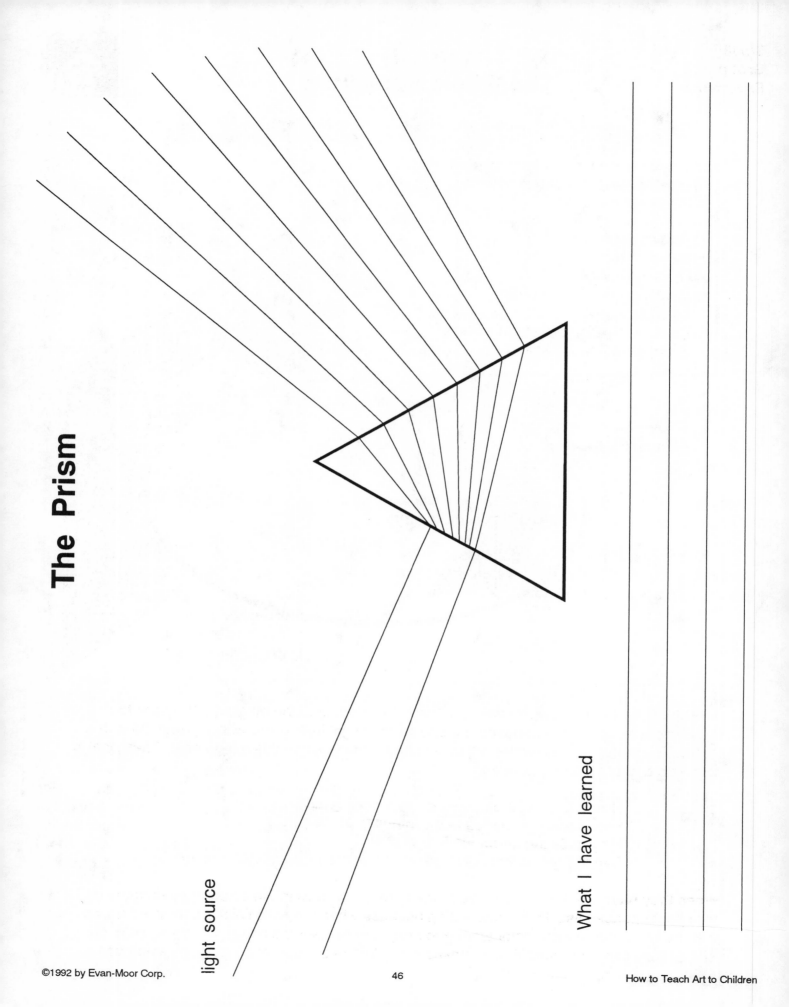

The Prism

light source

What I have learned

The Whole Sprectrum

Give students first-hand experience at creating their own rainbow of light.

Divide the class into groups of 4-5.
Each group will need:

• a tub of water
• a small mirror
• a flashlight
• a paper cone to concentrate
  the light
• Spectrum Colors worksheet
  on page 48

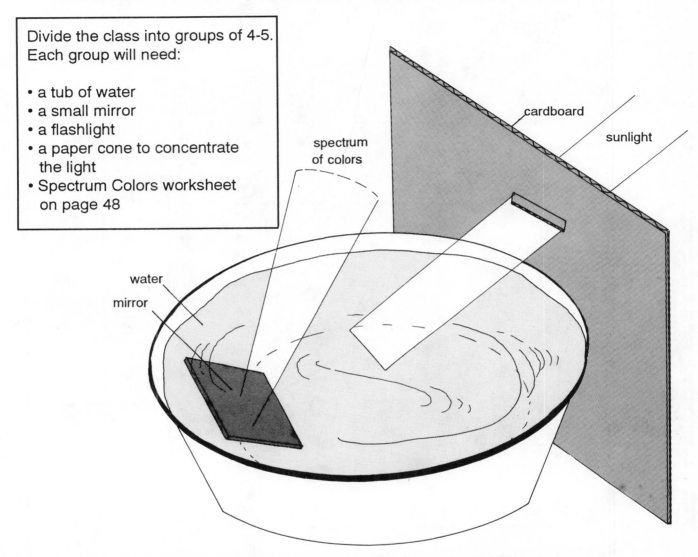

The students are to assemble their equipment according to the diagram. They are to experiment to see if they can create a spectrum of light just as the whole group did with a prism. The mirror and the water will substitute for the prism in this experiment. Their goal is to create a spectrum on the ceiling.

How many ways can they achieve their goal?
How could they increase the intensity of the colors?
Why does the mirror work as a prism?
Can the group think of another way to create a spectrum of light?

When they have created the spectrum, they are ready to fill in the colors they observe on the spectrum color list. This is interesting because when they are finished, they will notice that the first letter of each color word goes together to spell the name of a man...ROY G. BIV. If they can remember that, it makes the colors of the spectrum easy to remember.

How to Teach Art to Children

Spectrum

Fill in the blanks.

My name is

_____ _____ _____ _____ _____ _____ _____

How to Teach Art to Children

Prism Art

Students use what they have learned about the spectrum of colors to create a design.

Each student will need:
- 12 " x 18" (30.5 x 45.7 cm) sheet of white construction paper
- crayons or felt tip pens
- pencil

1. Students draw a triangle in the center of the art paper. This triangle represents a prism.

2. Beginning at the top, students lightly draw lines radiating out from the triangle. Each line design must be repeated eight times to create a section for each color in the color spectrum.

3. Students color in the design following the order the colors appear in the spectrum. Can they remember the correct order of colors? Did they learn about *Roy G. Biv*?

How to Teach Art to Children

Pattern and Design

Designs are made by using line, shape and color in interesting ways. Patterns are designs that are repeated several times.

• Repetition of Shapes, Lines or Colors..............................51

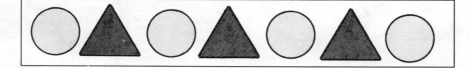

• Variation of Shapes and Sizes of Shapes.........................55

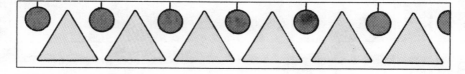

• Contrasting Colors in a Pattern 59

Repetition

Repetition of shapes, lines or colors is important
in planning a pattern. Use wrapping paper samples, end
papers inside literature books, wallpaper, etc. to demonstrate
how repetitive patterns of shapes, lines and colors can be
very useful in creating a pattern.

Set up a gadget printing center to explore patterns.
- Collect gadgets that offer simple shapes and lines.
  (forks, graters, whisks, etc.)
- Provide tempera paint in several colors.
- Have stacks of large inexpensive newsprint.

Begin by printing with all the gadgets in a random fashion.

Then try choosing one or two of the gadgets and plan a pattern that results
from repeating these two shapes over and over. Encourage student feedback.

Ask student input in trying other patterns using other gadgets assembled.

The gadgets and paint can remain in the corner of the room as a paint center
for students to use in exploring patterns and design.

• Literature References:

Rosie's Walk by Pat Hutchins;
Macmillan, 1971.
Examine the illustrations in this book to discover how many shapes and lines have been
used over and over to create patterned areas
within the picture. The artist has used mostly
warm colors in these illustrations. The limited
number of colors and the patterned areas
make these pages fun to share with students.

• Fine art examples to share with students:

Girl Before a Mirror
Pablo Picasso
This abstract picture of a girl uses many
reoccurring lines and shapes to create an
interesting design. Can you find the girl?

The Starry Night
Vincent Van Gogh
The landscape is comprised entirely of
repeating lines and shapes. The contrasting
colors and the pattern lend movement and
interest to this painting.

Patterned Rubbings

Divide the class into groups of 2-4 students.
Each group will need:

• construction paper
• cardboard
• scissors and glue
• newsprint
• crayons

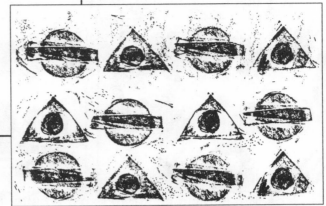

Students will work together to create a repetitive pattern
using geometric shapes of layered construction paper
pasted onto the cardboard. Building designs several
layers thick will add interest to the finished design.

When the design is complete and the glue has had time
to dry, the students will create rubbings of their textured
design in various color combinations. Provide students
with newsprint to experiment finding different color
combinations that please them.

This activity is especially useful during the holidays if the students
need a wrapping paper for gifts for parents.

How to Teach Art to Children

Sponge Painting

Students are asked to keep the concept of **repetition** of line, shape and color in mind when experimenting with sponge painting.

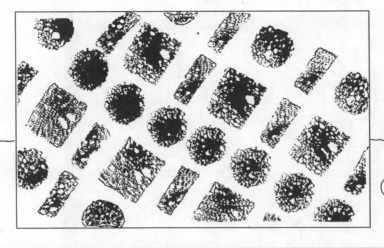

Each student will need:

• 9" x 12" (22.8 x 30.5 cm) newsprint
• tempera paint in a selection of colors
• sponges cut in basic shapes: squares, circles, triangles, hearts, etc.
• paper towels for blotting and clean-up

1. Students "warm-up" by experimenting with the various sponge shapes. They might begin by making a whole line or row of one shape. They might also try varying color so that they can see which colors work well together. Encourage them to try several practice pages.

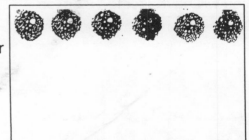

2. When students are ready to begin a painting they would like to keep, they may use art drawing paper instead of newsprint. The finished design may be a pattern made of shapes or it may be an actual picture using the sponge shapes as a part of the picture.

Students may enjoy comparing their sponge paintings with this artist's work.
La Négresse
Henri Matisse
This is an abstract portrait that was made by using repeating shapes and colors along with black line illustration.

Pattern Experiment

How many patterns can we make? Let's experiment
with lines and shapes and see!

Each student will need:
• 9" x 12" (22.8 x 30.5 cm) white construction paper
• crayons or felt pens

1. Fold the construction paper three times.
You will have created 8 boxes.

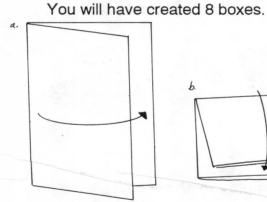

2. Make a different pattern in each box
using crayons or felt pens. Make sure students know how to create many types of
lines:

     wavy
     diagonal stripes
     polka-dots
     plaid
     checks
     angular

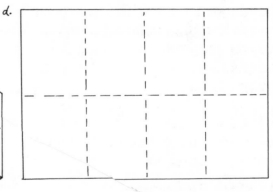

Variation

Variation of shapes and sizes of shapes contribute
to the creation of interesting designs.

Organize materials for a design center in your classroom. Share these materials in the beginning with your class. Illustrate for them the basic design objectives to which you want them to exposed:

- **repetition** of shape and color is important

- **variation** of shapes adds interest

- **overlapping** shapes

Materials:

- a flannel board
- basic felt shapes cut in 3 different sizes
  and in the three primary colors
  (circle, square, triangle, rectangle)

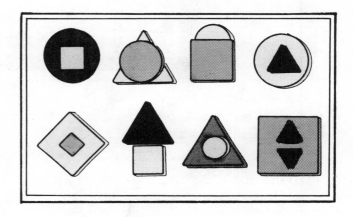

Challenge: Students will "play" with the felt shapes to create abstract designs. They should experiment with many different designs to see which ones they like the best.

Follow-up: Students are to recreate the design they develop onto a sheet of art paper with crayons.

• Literature References:

Thump, Thump, Rat-aTat-Tat by Gene Baer, illustrated by Lois Ehlert; Harper & Row, 1989. This book offers an opportunity to examine illustrations made up of basic shapes and electric colors. What a rich example of beautiful color and superb designing!

The Patchwork Quilt by Valerie Flournoy, illustrated by Jerry Pinkney; Dial Books, 1985. Beautiful patterning and design examples, rich colors and a sensitive story make this a book not to be missed.

• Fine art examples to share with students:

Adele Bloch-Bauer
Gustsav Klimt
Examine the background of this portrait carefully. It is a fine example of the three design principles of repetition of shape and color, variation and overlapping of shapes.

Pianist and Checker Players
Henri Matisse
Enjoy the many beautiful designs in this painting. Ask students to imagine this painting without patterns and designs. Would the impact be the same?

How to Teach Art to Children

Design a Banner

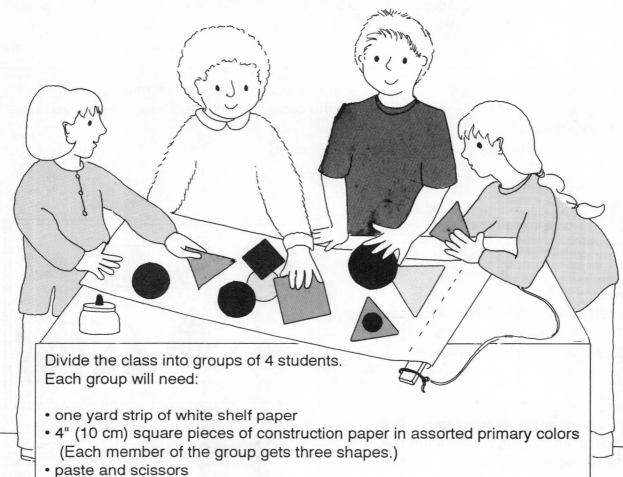

Divide the class into groups of 4 students.
Each group will need:

- one yard strip of white shelf paper
- 4" (10 cm) square pieces of construction paper in assorted primary colors
  (Each member of the group gets three shapes.)
- paste and scissors
- a yardstick and string

1. Students each pick out the three colors of construction
paper squares they prefer.

2. They must decide on the shapes they want to contribute
to the banner design. They cut one shape from each of
the squares.

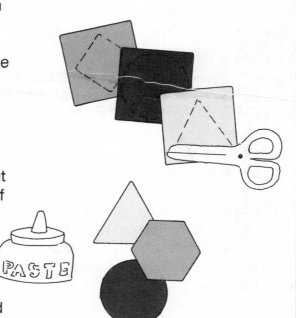

3. They place the shelf paper in the middle of the table
and they each take a turn placing one of their shapes on
the banner. They may not move anyone else's shape, but
they can overlap another shape. They continue until all of
the group's shapes are on the shelf paper.

4. Paste the shapes to the shelf paper.

5. Turn under one end of the shelf paper and staple.
Insert the yard stick and tie the yard around the ends and
hang up the banner to be admired by the rest of the class.

How to Teach Art to Children

Print a Design

Students use potato printing to apply what they have learned about elements of pattern and design. Set up a printing center in your room so that students have an opportunity to spend time experimenting with different designs.

1. Plan a design.
2. Pick shapes.
3. Pick colors.
4. Print it.

red   blue   yellow

Materials:

- tempera paint in several colors
- paper towels for blotting
- lots of newsprint or newspaper to use for trying out different designs
- vegetables in several shapes and sizes:
  - a potato sliced to a square shape and one cut as a triangle
  - half an apple
  - a carrot slice
  - a hunk of celery

Provide students with a list of challenges to follow:

- Plan a design where you use all of the available shapes.

- Plan a design where you use only two shapes.

- Create a diagonal design with a repeating pattern.

- Divide your paper into fourths, use the same shapes in a different way in each section.

- Plan a design in which you only use objects with rounded edges.

- Plan a design that is mostly angles: squares and triangles.

How to Teach Art to Children

Design a Painting

Set up a paint center at an easel where students can create an abstract painting.

This painting center will have two sections:

1. One section is a planning area where students have access to construction paper scraps, paste and scissors. This is where they can create small "thumbnail" plans of what their large painting will be. When they have designed a plan they are happy with, they can move to the paint area and begin.

scrap box

2. In the paint area, provide them with large paint paper, colored tempera with several palette choices, and both wide and narrow brushes. When the students come to this area, they tape their small "thumbnail plan" to the corner of the easel so they can refer to it as they paint.

How to Teach Art to Children

Contrasting Colors

The use of contrasting colors in a pattern strengthens the design.

After discussing literature and fine art examples with the class, it is time to explore and experiment with a design using different color schemes. This large group lesson is really a chance to just have a good time with designs.

Each student will need:
• 9" x 12" (22.8 x 30.5 cm) white art paper
• felt pens in several colors
• pencil

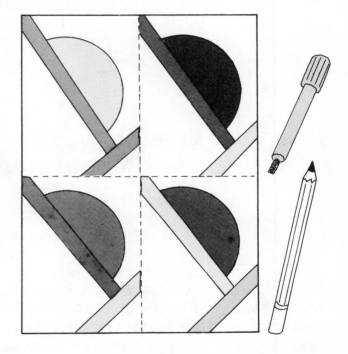

1. Students fold their paper into quarters.
2. They plan a design they like in the first box and lightly sketch it in with a pencil. Then they pencil that same design in each of the four boxes.
3. The challenge is to add color to each of these designs in a different way. Suggest that they try using a different color scheme in each box.

When the class has finished, discuss what they have discovered from this experience. Have they developed some preferences for certain color schemes or combinations?

• **Literature References:**

Tree of Cranes by Allen Say; Houghton Mifflin, l991.
Every page in this book is an example of simple, yet balanced design. The kite in the story has intricate patterns and contrasting colors. Students will enjoy sharing the charm and beauty of this book.

Her Seven Brothers by Paul Goble; Bradbury Press, 1988.
Each book that Paul Goble illustrates is full of beautiful designs and patterns to share with students. This one is a good example. These illustrations will inspire students to try new patterns in their own artwork. His use of contrasting colors adds sparkle to every page.

• **Fine art examples to share with students:**

Homage to the Square: Broad Call
Josef Albers
This design is done in only one color (a red) and using only one shape (a square).

Simultaneous Counter-Composition
Theo van Doesburg
Compare Albers' painting to this design that uses contrasting colors and several different shapes.

The Aero
Marsden Hartley
Ask students what they like about this design. What design elements has this artist followed?

Colorful Choices

Everyone uses the same pattern but develops a
different color scheme.

Divide the class into groups of 2-4 students.
Each group will need:

• construction paper scraps in all colors
• 6" x 18" (15 x 45.7 cm) strips of construction paper in assorted colors
• a Color Choice Chart (page 61)
• paste and scissors

1. The teacher draws the pattern for the day on the chalkboard.

2. Tell each group that it is their challenge to create four copies of your design but in new
interesting color combinations. Encourage them to experiment using some of the color combinations listed on the Color Choice Chart.

How to Teach Art to Children

Color this form before using.

Color Choice Chart

Choose a palette to use on your design.

1. Primary colors	**2. Secondary colors**
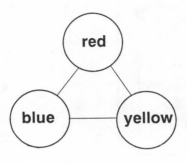	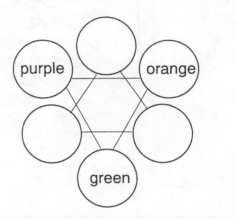
3. Complementary colors	**4. Black, white plus an accent color**
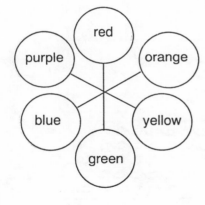	
5. Warm colors	**6. Cool colors**
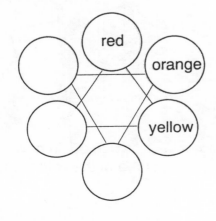	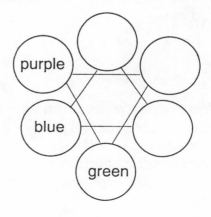

How to Teach Art to Children

Match the Design

Wallpaper and wrapping paper come in interesting patterns.
Let students use these as the beginning for a design of their own.

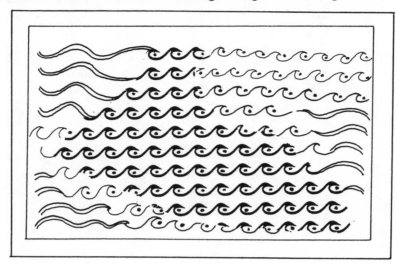

Materials:
- assorted wrapping paper or wallpaper designs
- large construction paper
- felt pens and crayons
- paste

1. Students rip off a piece of wrapping paper or wallpaper that has an element of design that they find interesting. They paste this sample somewhere on a piece of construction paper.

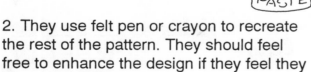

2. They use felt pen or crayon to recreate the rest of the pattern. They should feel free to enhance the design if they feel they have a good idea.

3. Frame the finished picture with a contrasting color construction paper.

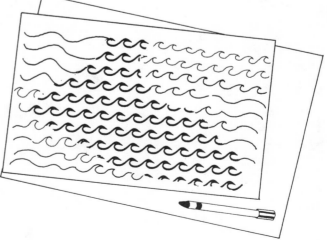

How to Teach Art to Children

Lines and Shapes

Lines of All Kinds...64

Curves and Angles...68

Lines Outline Shapes 71

Lines of All Kinds

Lines have names that describe their place in space. They may be diagonal, vertical or horizontal. These types of lines may be thick or thin, solid or broken. When two of these lines sit next to each other they become parallel lines.

Explain to students that we find lines everywhere. Have them look at their environment and name all of the lines that can be seen in our world.

Lines in leaves, fences, tree trunks, horizons, etc.

Introduce the vocabulary *diagonal*, *vertical* and *horizontal* as ways of describing lines in space. Look about the classroom and search for examples of each type.

Reproduce for students the Lines form on page 65.
Students begin by drawing one line of each type in the area indicated.

Then return to each box and draw another line alongside each of the original lines. They have now created parallel lines.

Ask them to shade in the area between the two parallel lines. Now they have created a thick line out of two thin lines.

Finally, have students draw broken lines in each of the areas. The broken lines may be slotted or dotted.

Students complete this lesson by adding more lines to complete a design. They may also want to add color to their designs.

• Literature References:

Drummer Hoff adapted by Barbara Emberly and illustrated by Ed Emberly; Prentice-Hall, 1967.
Students are challenged visually by the bold outline of shapes and the interesting way line is used inside objects. Encourage them to look for the way the artist has used line to enhance these illustrations.

• Fine art examples to share with students:

Sun
David Hockney
The artist has used lines in an interesting way in this still life painting. How many kinds of lines do you recognize?
Stairway at 48 Rue de Lille, Paris
Edward Hopper
Hopper's work is rich with strong line images. This painting makes an impression because of his design using lines to move your eye through the painting.

         How to Teach Art to Children

Lines

Lines have names that describe their place in space.

---

diagonal

---

vertical

---

horizontal

Line Designs

Reinforce what students have learned about vertical, horizontal
and diagonal lines by giving them an opportunity to talk together
and plan a design using these elements.

Divide the class into groups of 2-4 students.
Each group will need:

- shelf paper cut in a one yard (91 cm) length
- 1/2" x 12" (1.3 x 30.5 cm) construction paper strips in assorted colors
- 1" x 12" (2.5 x 30.5 cm) construction paper strips in assorted colors
- felt tip pens
- paste and scissors

Students divide their piece of shelf paper into
three areas using black felt tip pen.
These areas may be any configuration the
group prefers: squares, overlapping shapes,
etc.

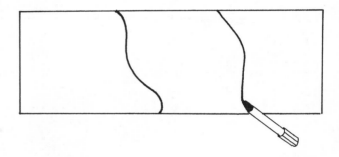

The design in each area will be created by
pasting down the paper strips in various colors.
One area will contain only horizontal lines.
These lines may be thick, thin, solid or broken.
Lay the paper strips down, trim off the excess,
discuss the effect and then paste them in place.

Fill in the other two areas. Create a vertical
design in one and diagonal design in the other.

Now add felt tip pen color to enrich each design. Students may choose to add color on the
paper strips or in-between the strips.

The Mystery Line Paint Center

Prepare a paint area where the following
materials are available:

• tempera paint in bright colors
• wide and narrow brushes
• large painting paper

1. You need to prepare the paper before the students come to the
paint center. Each paper needs one line drawn on it with a wide
felt tip pen. The line may be a vertical, horizontal or diagonal.

2. The student chooses the paper of his/her choice and finishes
the line design at the paint center. Encourage students to use as
many types of lines as possible in this project.

                                                                                       How to Teach Art to Children

Curves and Angles

Lines can be bent into curves and broken into angles. In this way, lines create an infinite number of configurations.

Using the chalkboard, brainstorm all of the different types of lines that can be created by changing a regular straight line into one that bends or curves.

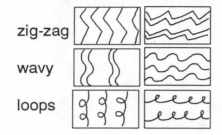

zig-zag

wavy

loops

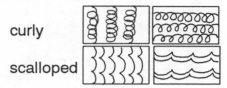

curly

scalloped

etc.

Give each student a 9" x 12" (22.8 x 30.5 cm) sheet of construction paper. Have them fold the paper into eight squares. Invite them to create a different type of line in each box. These lines be vertical, horizontal or diagonal.

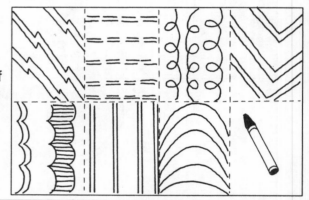

• Literature References:

Ten Little Rabbits by Virginia Grossman & Sylvia Long; Chronicle Books, 1991.
How has line added to the beauty of this book? The designs in the blankets and clothing of the rabbits show a use of lines angles and colors to create beautiful designs.

The Girl Who Loved Wild Horses by Paul Goble; Dutton, 1978.
Compare the illustrations in this book with the ones in the previous book. What theme do they both follow? What similarities and differences can students detect in the use of curves and angles?

• Fine art examples to share with students:

Rush Hour, New York
Max Weber
The use of angles and lines bending in many directions gives the impression of a busy, noisy city.

The Tiger
Granz Marc
Marc has created a powerful image from angles and lines. The angles and the strong primary and secondary colors portray an animal that is usually represented with rounder, curvier lines. Why did the artist choose to use these lines?

How to Teach Art to Children

Curved or Bent

Students benefit from having a time to discuss with other students the different types of lines they have learned about and how they like to combine these into interesting designs.

Divide the class into groups of 3 students.
Each group will need:

• 6" square (15 cm) pieces of white construction paper
• 12" x 18" (30.5 x 45.7 cm) black construction paper
• crayons or felt pens

Each student gets two squares of white construction paper. The challenge is to use crayon or felt pen to create two line designs:
    • one using bent, angular lines
    • one using curved lines
They may use any color combination they wish.

After all the students in the group have finished their designs, the students group their designs together on the large black construction paper and paste them down. They must decide how these designs should fit together and how they might be organized on the paper.

How to Teach Art to Children

Line Delight

Challenge students to create a design beginning with two lines. These lines drawn with black felt pen may be horizontal, vertical or diagonal. BUT both lines must travel in the same direction. The lines do not need to be parallel. One line may be curved and the other line bent. After establishing these two lines, the student may add as many other types and colors of lines as he/she chooses.

Step 1: Provide students with newsprint and have them work out three or four different designs following the challenge of this assignment. Ask students to share with you and others how they feel about these sketches and which one they would like to develop into a finished picture.

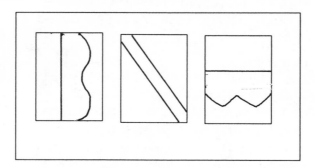

Step 2: Students go to the paint center and create the design they have chosen. Now they will be adding color to their design. Which color combinations will work the best?

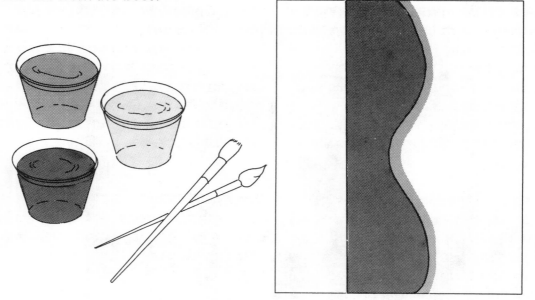

Lines Outline Shapes

Students have had experience with many types of lines. Now they will see that lines have another characteristic. Lines create the outline of shapes.

As we investigate these shapes, we discover that every time a line outlines a shape, it is really creating two images: the positive one we have outlined and the negative one that is the background.

1. Provide each student with newsprint and ask them to sketch along with you.
   Draw a circle, a square and a triangle.
   Each of these shapes is made up of curved and bent lines.
   These are basic shapes that we see all the time, but now we can see that they are all created out of line.

2. Let's look at simple objects and see what kind of a line outlines these shapes (apple, bottle or a vase). This form of drawing is called **contour** or outline drawing.

We look carefully at the object as we draw it on our paper; we only draw what we see as the outline of this object. We don't draw any inside details. Try not picking your pencil up as you draw the outline. The resulting drawing may be distorted and exaggerated but it emphasizes that form is an outline in space and we can manipulate that form as we draw. This lesson may be practiced often as we attempt more and more complicated subjects.

• **Literature References:**	• **Fine art examples to share with students:**
Why Mosquitoes Buss in People's Ears retold by Verna Aardema, illustrated by Leo and Diane Dillon; Dial, 1975. Examine the way the illustrator has used white line to outline shapes. The animals and the objects in the background are broken down into smaller shapes and pieces. Notice how well it all holds together despite the sectioning.	*Boy in Sailor Suit with Butterfly Net* Pablo Picasso This abstract painting of a young boy is distorted and exaggerated. It has the flavor of a contour drawing. This work, however, has had detail added to the inside of the figure. Students might enjoy comparing their efforts at contour work with that of a famous painter.
Truck by Donald Crews; Greenwillow, 1980. This illustrator has chosen to use very simple outlines of shapes to illustrate this book. Compare the differences in the shapes of the foreground and the shapes of the background. How are they different? Why are these illustrations so attractive?	*The Old King* *Georges* Rouault Rouault often used black to outline the basic shapes in his pictures and give a stained glass effect to his work.

How to Teach Art to Children

Positive and Negative Shapes

As we investigate shapes, we discover that every time a line outlines a shape, it is really creating two images: the positive one we
have outlined and the negative one that is the background. Take a
square of construction paper and cut out a circle in the center. Now
you really have **two** circles: the **positive** one you cut out and the
negative space that was left.

Divide the class into groups of 2-4 students.
Each group will need:

- construction paper cut into 6" (15 cm) squares
  (provide colors that have strong contrast)
- paste and scissors
- felt tip pens

1. Give each student in the group one piece of paper.
They are to fold the square and cut a shape out of the center.
Now they have a positive and a negative representation of that
same shape.

2. They trade their positive shape with someone in their group.

3. Then each person chooses a piece of construction paper in a
contrasting color to use as a background sheet. They paste their
positive and negative shape on the background in an interesting
manner.

4. They can add further design elements with felt pens.

5. Put up all of the groups' work on the bulletin board and enjoy the
different combinations.

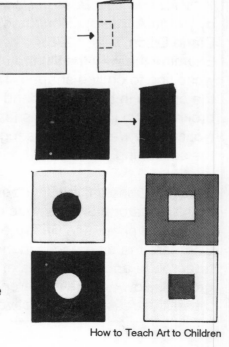

Shape Designs

Let's create large, bold designs by outlining a shape
and adding a patterned design in the positive area.

Materials:

- 12" x 18" (30.5 x 45.7 cm) white construction paper
- 12" x 18" (30.5 x 45.7 cm) construction paper in
  assorted colors
- paste and scissors
- crayon or felt pen

1. Students draw a large shape on the white construction paper
with a black felt pen. (They may want to sketch the line first
with a pencil.) The shape may be just a circle, square or triangle or it may be a more complicated contour drawing.

2. Cut out the shape on the outside of the felt pen line.

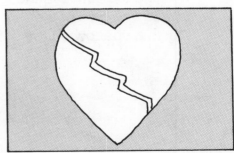

3. Paste the shape in the center of the chosen color of
construction paper.

4. Create a pattern inside the shape.

How to Teach Art to Children

Shading Shapes

Students will discover that you can convey solidarity to shapes with shading and color.

> Read:
> *Shapes* by Philip Yenawine; The Museum of Modern Art, N. Y., Delacorte Press, 1991. This book will give you and your students insight into how basic shapes go together to create more complicated shapes in our world.

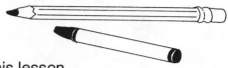

Students can use pencils, crayons and newsprint in this lesson. They will use shading and color to create shapes that occupy space.

Draw a ball.
Pretend the sun is in the top left corner.
Shade the bottom half.
Lay in a shadow on the ground.

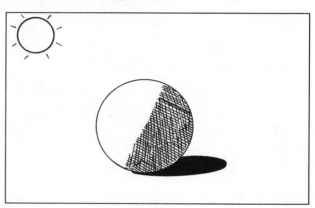

Draw a box.
Pretend the sun is in the top right hand corner.
Shade one side of the box.
Lay in a shadow on the ground.

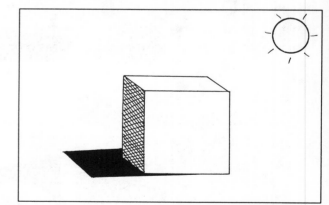

Make the box into a house.
Put a sun in the sky.
Shade the dark side of the house.
Lay in a shadow.
Draw a ball in the yard.
Which way will the shadow go?

How to Teach Art to Children

Texture

- Awareness of Texture 76

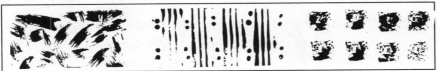

- Repetition Creates Texture 81

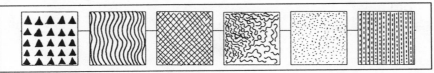

- Creating Texture with Paint 85

- Collage has Texture 89

How to Teach Art to Children

Awareness of Texture

The world is full of a variety of textures. Children have first-hand experiences with many textures. They know about rough rocks and smooth marbles. They respond to the concept of touching and describing the world on the basis of what they see and feel. Texture needs to be sensed by students in many three-dimensional forms before we learn about the possibility of representing texture two-dimensionally.

Let's investigate our world together. What can we see and touch that we can describe in terms of how it looks and feels? Sometimes it helps to think in terms of opposites when compiling the list.

• Brainstorm lists of vocabulary.

wooly	smooth
soft	rough
hard	bumpy
prickly	fluffy
slick	sticky
ragged	corrugated

• Using 5" (13 cm) squares of paper, do rubbings of different textures around the room. Identify each rubbing as bumpy, rough, smooth, etc. Compile all students' work on a sheet of butcher paper.

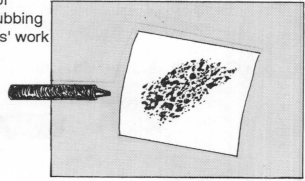

• Categorize all rubbings as man-made surfaces or natural.

• Literature References:

The Great Kapok Tree by Lynne Cherry; Harcourt Brace Jovanovich, 1990.
Invite students to examine the techniques the illustrator has used to create the textured look of the jungle foliage and the animal coverings.

Home Place by Crescent Dragonwagon, illustrated by Jerry Pinkney; Macmillan, 1990.
Compare Jerry Pinkney's technique in painting trees and animals to that of Lynne Cherry. How does he create the impression of texture?

• Fine art examples to share with students:

Picking Flowers
Auguste Renoir
Renoir creates a landscape full of light and the brightness of blooming flowers. The forms are fuzzy because of the "dappled" effect but the result is one rich in depth and texture.

The Blank Signature
René Magritte
This painting has richly textured trees and grass. The subject matter is interesting because it is a surrealistic view of a rider in a forest. Why did the artist use this approach? Share other Magritte paintings with students.

How to Teach Art to Children

Sharing Textures

Give students time to experiment with textures. The end result will be crayon rubbings that have interesting color combinations and different textured effects.

Divide the class into groups of 2-4 students.
Each group will need:

- 24"(61 cm) square sheet of colored butcher paper
    (folded into 16 squares)
- 5" (13 cm) squares of white construction paper
    (16 per group)
- crayons and paste
- Plan a Rubbing form (page 78)
- assortment of surfaces with interesting textures
    (sandpaper, bark, graters, or other textures
    available around the school, etc.)

Plan a Rubbing

1. Choose three textures: _____
   _____
   _____

2. Choose a color palette
   ☐ primary colors _____ ☐ cool _____
   ☐ secondary colors _____ ☐ warm _____
   ☐ complementary colors _____ ☐ other: _____

3. Divide the paper into 16 squares. Now begin the rubbings to place in these squares.

4. Everyone in the group takes a little square of paper. What texture do you want to show on this paper? Pick a crayon in the color scheme the group has chosen and make a rubbing.

5. Put all of the papers on the big chart. Put one in each box. Move the textures around until the group decides it is the way you want it. Paste the boxes in place.

Students will work in groups and make decisions about their rubbing job before they begin. They record those decisions on their Plan a Rubbing form. Then they begin the job of locating the textured surfaces that they want to use.

Students may share this experience in many different ways:

- The group must come to an agreement on the textures and the colors they will use.

- They must decide on how to share the actual rubbing so that each member of the group can contribute.

- They must agree on where to place the rubbings on the chart before pasting them in place.

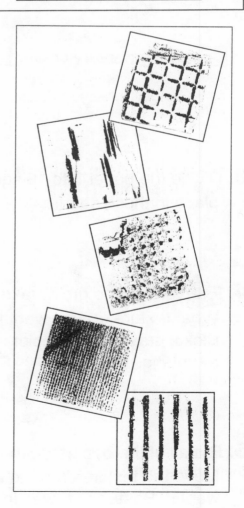

Plan a Rubbing

1. Choose three textures: _____

_____

_____

2. Choose a color palette

☐ primary colors _____   ☐ cool _____

_____   _____

_____   _____

☐ secondary colors _____   ☐ warm _____

_____   _____

_____   _____

☐ complementary colors _____   ☐ other: _____

_____   _____

_____   _____

3. Divide the paper into 16 squares. Now begin the rubbings to place in these squares.

4. Everyone in the group takes a little square of paper.
What texture do you want to show on this paper?
Pick a crayon in the color scheme the group has chosen and make a rubbing.

5. Put all of the papers on the big chart. Put one in each box.
Move the textures around until the group decides it is the way you want it. Paste the boxes in place.

 How to Teach Art to Children

On the Street Where I Live

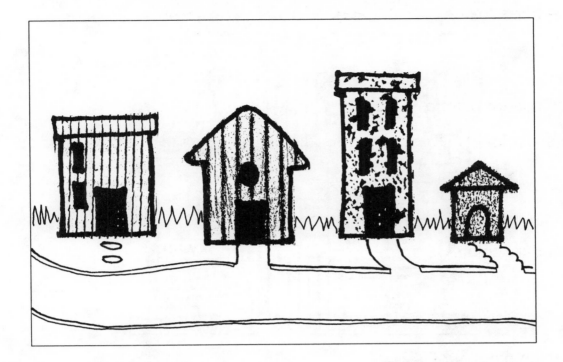

Each student will need:
• 12" x 18" (30.5 x 45.7 cm) piece of white construction paper
• crayons
• pencil
• felt pen

1. Students do simple pencil drawings of several houses in a row. Create areas large enough to have room to do rubbings inside lines.

2. Then they do crayon rubbings to create the inside area of each building.

3. They outline the buildings and add details with black crayon or felt pen.

Corrugated Texture

Each student gets his/her own square of corrugated paper and white construction paper to create a textured crayon picture emphasizing the strong vertical lines in the corrugated paper.

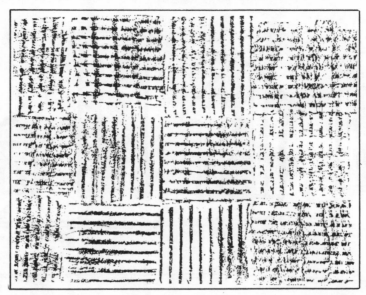

Each student needs:
• 9" x 12" (22.8 x 30.5 cm) white construction paper
• 3" x 5" (7.5 x 13 cm) strip of corrugated paper
• crayons

Steps to follow:

1. Place the corrugated paper below the construction paper and rub with the side of a crayon.

2. Move the corrugated paper and rub again. Continue this process until the design is complete.

Help students realize that they have several options:

1. They can rub the corrugated paper in different directions.

2. They can use a limited palette, complementary colors or any combination of color they like.

3. They can do a controlled, regular, even design or a loose, flowing one.

How to Teach Art to Children

Repetition Creates Texture

Texture can be created in pictures by using repetition of lines and shapes. This repetition creates a kind of rhythm that holds the pattern together

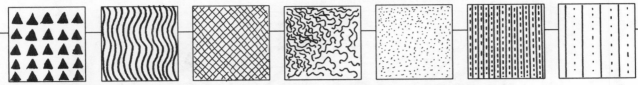

1. Discuss how different textures can be created by repeating a pattern.

- One shape repeated over and over fills an area and creates a patterned effect.

- Wavy lines create movement and texture.

- Cross-hatching adds shading and texture.

- Squiggles can be close together or far apart.

- Stippling can be very controlled and exacting.

- Lines can be repeated in many variations.
  Lines and shapes repeated close together create a dark effect.
  Lines and shapes repeated farther apart create a lighter effect.

2. Give each student a 3" square (7.5 cm) of white construction paper. They use a black crayon to create a textured effect with a repeated line or shape. Lay all of the students' squares together and tape them together with cellophane tape.

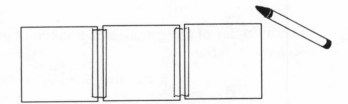

- **Literature References:**

The Midnight Farm by Reeve Lindbergh, illustrated by Susan Jeffers; Dial Books, 1987. The use of cross-hatching and repetitive designs to create pattern and shading is beautifully exemplified in this book. Each page offers students many examples of ways to create texture in their own work.

Mufaro's Beautiful Daughters by John Steptoe; Lothrop, Lee & Shepard, 1987. This book offers students another chance to compare illustration techniques. The way Steptoe creates texture in these pictures is similar to the crosshatching used by Jeffers.

- **Fine art examples to share with students:**

Woman in a Striped Dress
Edouard Vuillard
Why does this painting have the feel of detail that makes you remember it? The repetition of shapes and lines help to create the impression of texture.

Houses at Auvers
Vincent van Gogh
The repeated brush strokes on the roofs are especially effective in creating a bumpy, rough-looking surface. Students can appreciate how this artist has used repetitive shape and brush strokes to develop a rich textured feeling in this landscape.

       How to Teach Art to Children

Nature's Textures

Explore textures in our world as a way of developing different techniques to use in our artwork.

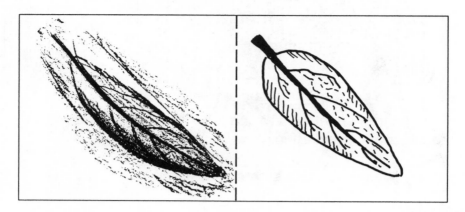

Divide the class into groups of 2-4 students.
Each group will need:

- items collected from nature (leaves, cactus, bark, rocks, etc.)
- items with texture that are man-made (baskets, woodwork, metal grates, etc.).
- 3" x 6" (7.5 x 15 cm) white art paper
- crayons

Each member of the group gets a piece of art paper and folds it in half.

They use their crayons to make a rubbing of one of the available textures on one side of the folded paper. They pass that paper to another member of the group.

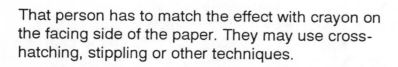

That person has to match the effect with crayon on the facing side of the paper. They may use cross-hatching, stippling or other techniques.

How to Teach Art to Children

Textured Abstract Still Life

Each student will need:

- 9" x 12" (22.8 x 30.5 cm) white construction paper
- pencil and black felt pen
- colored pencils or felt pens

1. The teacher provides a set-up of a simple still life using fruits and vegetables. The students use pencil to do a rough sketch.

2. They outline the shapes with black felt pen.

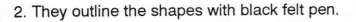

3. Colored pencils are used to add a different texture to each item in the still life. Encourage students to use as many different techniques as they can.

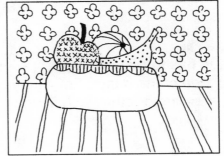

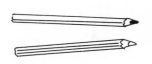

A Textured Landscape Mural

Set up a **Create a Mural** center in your room. Build the theme around an area of study in your classroom or link it with a piece of literature you are using with your students.

• Decide on a landscape theme that your class will illustrate:

forest   mountains
jungle   woods
desert   grasslands

• Pencil in the basic forms on a long sheet of butcher paper.

• Provide students with crayons, textured surfaces (corrugated paper, sandpaper, etc.).

• The challenge to the students is to create a different texture in each section. Encourage students to experiment with different combinations of lines and shapes or rubbed surfaces.

• Students may enjoy an additional challenge. They may do this lesson using a single texture techniques and a limited selection of colors.

    • primary colors only
    • warm and cool palettes
    • complementary colors
    • secondary colors

How to Teach Art to Children

Creating Texture with Paint

Investigate painting techniques that create textured effects. The ways of achieving these effects are many and varied. Students need to experiment to discover which effect works best for them.

Provide your class with a painting demonstration of techniques that lend texture to a painting. Create a chart as you go along to list all of the techniques you have tried. Leave this chart up in a painting center for students to use for reference. They may add to the chart the techniques they discover work for them.

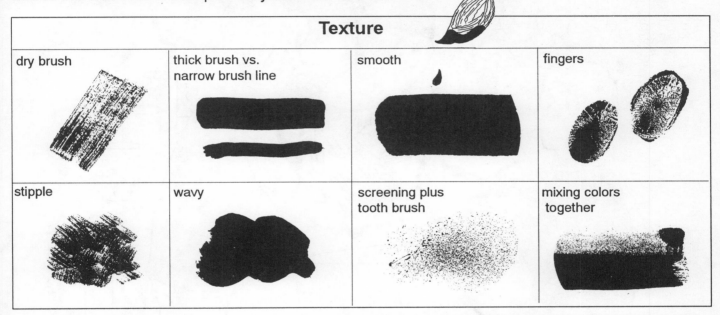

Texture

| dry brush | thick brush vs. narrow brush line | smooth | fingers |
| stipple | wavy | screening plus tooth brush | mixing colors together |

• **Literature References:**

The First Dog by Jan Brett; Harcourt Brace Jovanovich, 1988.
Brett creates fine detail in her paintings with techniques that students can appreciate. Many of the pages appear to use almost a sponge painting effect to create rough and rugged rocks.

Jack and the Beanstalk retold and illustrated by Lorinda Bryan Cauley; G. P. Putnam & Sons, 1983.
Examine Cauley's brush strokes to see which techniques help her achieve texture in her pictures. Students will recognize many of the techniques that they have already learned.

• **Fine art examples to share with students:**

Baby at Play
Thomas Eakins
Look at the textured effect in the background and the bricks in the foreground. Encourage students to examine how the artist has used his paint to achieve this feeling.

Pigeons
John Sloan
Compare the brick effect in this painting with the Eakins painting. How did this artist create the texture of bricks? What colors has he used?

How to Teach Art to Children

Cooperative Painting

Let's practice the techniques we have learned to create a textured effect with paint and reinforce positive social skills at the same time. Divide the class into groups of 4-5 students.

Each group needs:

• one large sheet of painting paper
• a paint jar for each person in the group
• a paintbrush for each person

The Challenge:

Each group is to cooperate and paint an abstract design of their choice. Each member of the group has a can of paint and his/her own brush. The ONLY rule is: you may not paint over another person's work. Each student creates textured effects moving around the paper until the whole paper is filled. After the paint has dried, hang up the paintings from the different groups and compare effects.

Print a Texture

Sponge, potato and gadget printing are wonderful tools for establishing texture and pattern in a picture. Let's experiment with them to see what they have to offer.

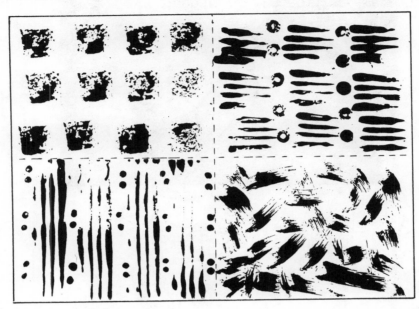

Each student will need:

- a 12" x 18" (30.5 x 45.7 cm) sheet of construction paper
- access to a printing center with sponges, potatoes and gadget printing equipment
- tempera paint in several colors

Steps to follow:

1. Fold the paper.

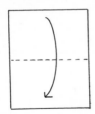

2. Create a different print pattern in each area using the colors of choice.

Options:
- Ask students to repeat each technique twice in the same painting.
- Restrict color use to two or three colors.
- Let students try different ways of folding their papers.
- Ask students to experiment. They might create a high contrast design in one picture and then do another design in muted tones.

How to Teach Art to Children

Scratch Away Texture

Each student will need:
- a 9" x 12" (22.8 x 30.5 cm) sheet of white art paper
- crayons
- plastic knives
- black tempera paint
- liquid detergent

Students design and complete a crayon picture on the theme of their choice. The crayon must be worked in solid, heavy blocks. Students should be encouraged to create designs with bold contrasting colors.

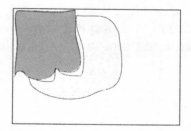

The completed crayon designs are then painted completely black with a mixture of the black paint and detergent.

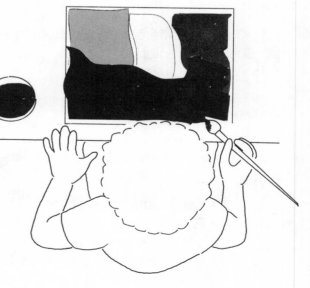

After the paint is completely dry, the paint is gently scratched away with a plastic knife to reveal the color below. The textures are created by the techniques used in scratching away the paint.
(This is a messy procedure. Cover table with newspaper to make clean-up easier.)

How to Teach Art to Children

Collage has Texture

texture

Collage is defined as a composition made by fixing pieces of paper, string, cloth, wallpaper, etc. to a surface. Let's provide students with the materials and time to explore this way of illustrating texture.

After looking at fine art and literature examples, we are about to discover how we can manipulate paper to create textured effects in our art projects.

Each student will need:
• two sheets of 9" x 12" (22.8 x 30.5 cm) construction paper (one each of two colors)
• one sheet of ditto paper
• scissors and paste

1. Students use one of the construction paper sheets as the background sheet.

2. They use the remaining construction paper and the bond paper as the material to be manipulated. The construction paper gives a rough effect, the bond paper a smooth one.

3. What can be done to paper to create texture? Let's experiment and see. Demonstrate the techniques listed here. Students will invent their own methods as you go along. When you are finished, paste the textured examples in an interesting manner onto the background sheet.

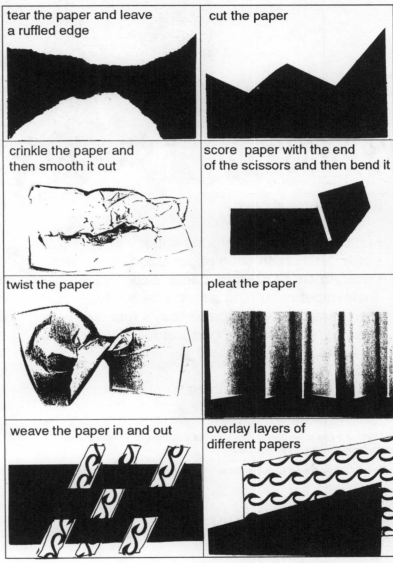

tear the paper and leave a ruffled edge

cut the paper

crinkle the paper and then smooth it out

score paper with the end of the scissors and then bend it

twist the paper

pleat the paper

weave the paper in and out

overlay layers of different papers

• Literature References:

We have a rich collection of collage examples in the books done by the following authors/ illustrators. They all exhibit how well this style works in creating colorful, textured illustrations.

    Leo Lioni
    Ezra Jack Keats
    Brian Wildsmith

• Fine art examples to share with students:

Mixed-Media
Kurt Schwitters
Schwitters (1887-1948) is often thought of as a leader in the art of collage. Look at his work and see what he has used to create interesting works of art with many different types of materials.

Texture a Tree

Groups of students cooperate in creating a stand of trees for the bulletin board. Each tree will incorporate some of the texture techniques they have already experienced. Divide the class into groups of 2-4 students.

Each group will need:

• butcher paper background sheet
• assorted construction paper colors and sizes
• assortment of unusual paper: paper bags, wallpaper, wrapping paper, tissue, etc.
• tempera paint in assorted colors (put out brushes, sponges and gadgets for application)
• crayons to use for rubbing
• scissors
• white glue thinned with water and a brush applicator

Many of these materials may be a part of a classroom art center and students can pick what they need.

Steps to follow:

1. Discuss with students the objective: each group is to create a tree utilizing as many texture techniques as they can. (See page 89.)
2. Brainstorm a list of the types of trees they might consider (below).
3. Each group plans their tree and gathers their materials. They will need to assign jobs and work together to complete the job.
4. The finished tree is cut out and pinned to the bulletin board.

Use an encyclopedia to gather more information on types and characteristics of all types of trees.

tree in blossom	evergreen tree with pine cones
fruit tree	cactus
winter tree	oak tree with acorns
spring tree	tall eucalyptus
summer tree	topiary tree

How to Teach Art to Children

My Personal Collage

Set up an art center with resources for students. They need time to practice the texture techniques they have learned in creating collages of their own.

Collect materials that might be used in collages. Ask students to check at home to see what they can contribute. Brainstorm suggestions of materials that might be interesting.

When all materials are available, set up a center with interesting papers, watered down glue, brushes, felt pens, crayons and scissors.

Remind students that they can:
- tear paper
- cut paper
- overlap patterns
- use paint plus a torn paper
- use pinking shears

Resources for Collage
- paper bags
- foil
- wallpaper
- wrapping paper
- rice paper
- colored papers
- packaging materials
- corrugated paper
- yarn
- cellophane
- tissue
- fabric
- 3-D items
- egg carton parts

1. Each student will need a 12" by 18" (22.8 x 30.5 cm) background sheet of construction paper or cardboard.

2. Students will pick the paper resources that interest them and then sit down to concentrate on the task of building a collage. You may want to direct student work towards a specific theme: underwater scene, landscape, cityscape, etc.

How to Teach Art to Children

Animal Collage

Let's create an animal collage. The same animal is done
twice; once as cut-paper design and again as a torn-paper.

Literature Resource:
Alexander and the Wind-up Mouse by
Leo Lioni: Pantheon, 1969. This delightful fable serves as an example of cut
versus torn-paper art. The "real" mouse
in this story is done with a torn-paper
edge. The mechanical mouse that be-
comes his friend is done with a cut-paper
edge. Both mice are the same design
except for the cut-torn technique.

Encourage students to compare the effect of torn-paper collage to cut paper. Children
tend to prefer cut paper because it is easier to control. The torn-paper edge, however,
is worth pursuing as a collage technique.

Materials:
• newsprint (any paper to use to make the patterns)
• 12" x 18" (30.5 x 45.7 cm) sheet of construction
paper for a background sheet
• construction paper in assorted sizes and colors
• wallpaper, wrapping paper, paper bags, etc.
• crayons and felt pens
• scissors
• white glue

Steps to follow:

1. Students choose an animal they want to
create. The following basic shape animals may
be used as a beginning. They draw the animal
shapes on a sheet of newsprint to use as a
pattern.

2. They trace the patterns on construction paper.
Each pattern must be traced twice. The color
choice will depend on what the animal is.

3. One set of shapes is cut out.
The other set of shapes is torn out.

4. The shapes are laid on a construction paper
background and glued in place.

5. Details are added with crayon or felt tip pen.

Cloth and Collage

texture

Cloth is a valuable resource to explore when making collages. Different patterns and textures give students the opportunity to create varied and interesting pieces.

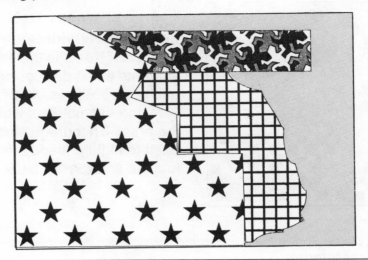

Materials:
• cloth scraps (as many colors, textures and patterns as possible)
• cardboard to use as a backing
• scissors that will cut cloth
• white glue diluted with water and a brush

Steps:

1. Place the materials in a center so students have the opportunity to browse and pick through the fabric to choose the combination of pieces they want to use together.

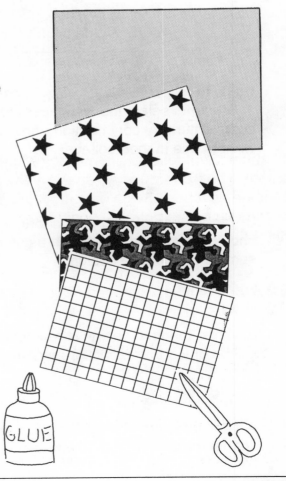

2. Students experiment with different arrangements of the fabric. They may want to try tearing as well as cutting to create pieces of an appropriate size. Patterns may overlap or weave in and out. Encourage students to experiment.

3. When the arrangement is complete, the pieces are brushed with diluted white glue and adhered to the cardboard.

4. Ragged edges may be controlled by placing the collage inside a paper frame after it is completed.

Wallpaper and Paint Create Texture

Combine wallpaper and tempera paint to create interesting collages.

Literature Resource:
Ezra Jack Keats is the illustrator to share with students when discussing the technique of paper and paint collages. All of his picture books are inspiring examples of what this medium can offer to the artist. Encourage students to see how he uses paint to highlight and add detail to the papers he has cut and torn as backgrounds.

Materials:
• wallpaper samples
• construction paper in assorted colors
• paint in several colors
• construction paper backgound sheets
• brushes, sponges and gadgets for printing
• glue diluted with water

Steps to follow:

1. Students select the wallpaper pieces and the complementary construction paper colors they want to use in their collage.

2. Techniques of cutting and tearing the papers should be experimented with as students assemble the collage design.

3. When the final design is ready, the wallpaper will be glued to the background sheet.

4. Now the student may add paint with a brush, sponge or printing tool to add detail.

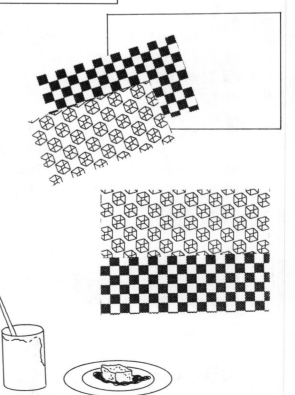

How to Teach Art to Children

Sandpaper and Paint Collage

Build in different textures to a painting by beginning
the design with pieces of sandpaper.

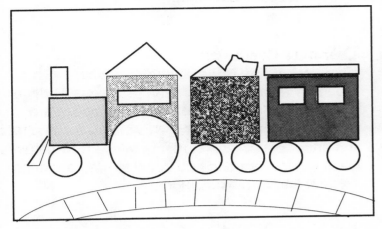

Fine art example to share with students:
Marked Man
Paul Klee
This abstract painting gives the textured look
of a sandpaper background. Sharing this
work of art with students might stimulate
ideas of how they might incorporate this
technique in their painting.

Materials:
• 3"(7.5 cm) sandpaper squares
   (in different textures)
• construction paper backing
• tempera paint in several colors
• sponges, brushes and gadgets for printing
• black felt pen
• glue

Steps to follow:

1. Students choose the sandpaper they will use and glue it in place on the backing sheet.

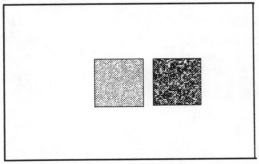

2. They add paint to the picture. They may use a brush, a sponge or a printing gadget.

3. Final details may be added with a black felt tip pen.

Useful Definitions

complementary colors- color pairs that sit opposite one another on the color wheel

hue- the colors of the color wheel

intensity- the brightness of a color

primary colors- colors which cannot be made by mixing other colors: red, yellow and blue

secondary colors- a color which is made by mixing two primary colors

shade- a variety of a particular color with black added

tertiary colors- a color which is made by mixing two secondary colors. These colors tend to be grayish.

tint- a variety of a particular color with white added

Unusual Color Word Vocabulary

lavender	pewter
puce	canary
powder blue	flesh
magenta	peach
fuchsia	maroon
charcoal	chartreuse
cyan	azure
sky blue	orchid
crimson	sienna
scarlet	cinnamon
hot pink	aquamarine
ocher	vermilion
mauve	olive
burnt umber	cerulean

Invite students to sort these according to the basic color categories. Keep a chart in the classroom so that you can add new ones as you learn about them.